Dr. & Mrs. Herbert L. Haney
92 Greenville Street
Newnan, GA 30263
P9-APQ-263

Published by Chartwell Books Inc.
A Division of Book Sales Inc.
110 Enterprise Avenue
Secaucus, New Jersey 07094

Printed and bound in Hong Kong
By Book Print International
Created and produced by
Sackett & Squire Ltd
2 Great Marlborough Street
London W.1.

Library of Congress 79-52748
ISBN 0 89009 284 2

Best Loved CATS OF THE WORLD

CHARTWELL BOOKS INC.

Best Loved

CATS OF THE WORLD

Peter McHoy

Contents

Introduction

Every year thousands of people open their homes to a new cat . . . and let in a creature that will have a profound impact on their lives for the next 12 years or so. They offer their homes and their hearts to a pet that will give endless hours of pleasure and delight; and yet it will always be its own master. The cat is an exquistively beautiful animal, and an affectionate and grateful pet — yet it will never surrender its independence and give you blind obedience.

Unlike a dog, a cat will only give you its love and obedience if you've earned it, and this is surely no bad thing. There is a tremendous satisfaction in learning to understand the minds and moods of our feline friends, and knowing that a happy relationship has been built upon this appreciation. In short, these beautiful creatures expect to be treated as equals — and usually are.

The cat is also a superbly designed animal — light and graceful, yet full of power and agility. The transition from a gentle purring ball of fur to a hunter ready to strike can be rapid and impressive. The accuracy of its leap and strike is deadly to the victim. The cat is a creature of lightning reaction.

Because most cats are now regarded as decorative pets rather than working animals, it's easy to forget that they were first domesticated because they are such efficient hunters.

It was almost certainly in Egypt that the cat's special relationship with man began. It would not have gone unnoticed that the wild cats were very adept at keeping rodents under control. And the cat proved its usefulness to man by preventing vast quantities of food stored in the granaries being destroyed by pests.

Such was the Egyptians' admiration for the cat that it became elevated to an object of religious significance. There are even legends of cats being used in ancient civilizations as guards — to protect warehouses and temples. This may seem far-fetched, but the cat was probably regarded with such veneration that it may have been sufficient to deter invaders from invoking the cat's wrath.

At different times, and in various cultures, these lovely creatures have fallen in and out of favour, sometimes being regarded as portenders of evil. Happily we live in more enlightened times, and the cat is valued throughout the world.

Over the centuries, many breeds have evolved, many from natural mutations, some as a direct consequence of the designs of man. The result is a variety of breeds to suit all tastes, each with its own unique characteristics. There are re-creations of the Egyptian Mau, long-haired Siamese, the strange-looking Rex cats, aristocratic Chinchillas, Ragdolls which are almost as dependent as babies, cats with lop ears, and even hairless cats, to mention just a few. Even among the popular longhairs there is a bewildering array of colors and forms, and the ubiquitous Tabby appears in brown, silver and red, in marbled, mackerel or spotted patterns.

All these, and many more of our best-loved or interesting breeds, are discussed in this book, many of them illustrated. Some are not universally available yet, but it would be a critical person indeed who could not readily find a cat to suit his personality and his pocket.

Chapter

1 Owning a Cat

Ask any cat owner why he likes cats and you'll soon realize that the cat is a creature of many parts. You'll be told the cat is intelligent, aristocratic or wild in appearance depending on mood, affectionate yet independent, full of character and inscrutable personality, but above all, a creature of grace and beauty. No wonder then that so many families choose to have a cat about the house.

Too often, however, we take these fascinating creatures for granted because they are such popular and widespread pets. We may even neglect them unintentionally simply because we have not always taken the trouble to understand them. Experience doesn't come without practice (and a little trial and error), but some things have to be right first time. If you realize your pet doesn't seem enthusiastic about the new wicker bed you've bought, because it doesn't offer much protection against draughts, you can buy a different bed. But if you choose the wrong cat the situation is more serious.

This chapter cannot provide a guaranteed way of making the right choice for, as with humans, the most unlikely combinations sometimes make an ideal match. But it will set you on the right lines, and take you through the first exciting months when you are getting to know each other.

If you're about to buy your first cat, remember that even the most expert and exalted exhibitor or breeder of cats was a beginner once. The fact that they have since aspired to such achievements is testimony that the rewards of a close understanding between cat and man are great for both. But it must also serve as a warning that once you own your first cat there is no knowing where it might end!

Left: these two Siamese kittens display all the impish alertness that makes kittens of all breeds so enchanting. Cats, such as the Siamese, which need a lot of attention are often best bought in pairs. They enjoy the extra companionship.

Above: like the three Tabby kittens on the old tree stump, these young Silver Tabbies show the typical M-mark on the forehead.

Above left: although individual kittens are delightful, they are at their most fascinating when playing or exploring with their litter-mates.

Owning a Cat

The excitement which naturally accompanies any decision to acquire something new should never be suppressed, but sometimes it's wise to temper it with a little caution. It's entirely natural to want to see your new pet ensconced cosily in your own home, and the temptation is to go out at once and return with a lovely kitten — just a ball of fur — in a cardboard box. But restraint is more vital now than at any other time. Remember, you are taking on a commitment for perhaps the next 15 years. Equally important, once you've bought your pet it's no use deciding that you prefer some other breed you've only just discovered.

Select your new pet with as much care and thought as you would a new car — with more, if anything, as it's likely to be with you for longer. Once you are quite certain you are ready to have your life taken over by a cat, then deciding on the right breed and shopping around for it need not be a burdensome chore; as with any interest or hobby, anticipation can be almost thrilling as the actual action.

Before even considering the *type* of cat you fancy, however, you need to be sure you fully appreciate the pros and cons of owning a cat: the difficulties as well as the joys.

Make no mistake, cats do need attention . . . lots of loving attention. Be prepared to spend time talking to your pet each day, and demonstrate affection. It will be well rewarded.

Cats' sex lives can be an embarrassment if not neutered. They like to be very active in this direction, which can lead to problems all round (few cats will stay indoors and silent while in heat). The outcome will be either unwanted kittens or a frustrated cat, neither of which is desirable. So unless you intend to go in for breeding (and that makes its own demands) you must be prepared to face up to your responsibilities and have your pet neutered. This is a straightforward operation and will cause little distress.

As with most pets, vacations will involve special arrangements (and probably additional expense).

If you have no garden and your pet has to be kept indoors most of the time, it will be necessary to keep him active to ensure he receives sufficient exercise. It also means litter trays will be required — and as cats are very fastidious these will need constant changing if they are to be used.

Long-haired cats need grooming — regularly. Do not underestimate this job; it should be a pleasurable experience for you both, but if your lifestyle is hectic and you don't have the time it can become an unwelcome chore.

If you haven't been deterred by now (and if you're an animal lover you will still be as keen as ever), then you can dwell on the advantages of having a cat as a pet — and there are many of them.

There is no need to be dragged out on a cold winter's morning to exercise your pet on a leash (though some breeds can be trained to walk on a leash) as with dogs.

Cats will adapt to a varied diet and they are not expensive to feed.

Provided they have been neutered, cats are likely to be quiet and peaceful pets.

They are very clean and easily housetrained — in fact you are unlikely to find a better pet in this respect.

Taking a cat into your home involves much more than with buying a hamster or a rabbit. You will have to share your home and life with him, so it's important to ask yourself how he is likely to settle in with other members of the household — whether animal or human.

An adult can cope with a new pet but children can be a little more unpredictable. There are very few children who don't like cats, but it is their very enthusiasm that can occasionally be a problem — play can be a little too rough. It all depends on the age and personality of the child. Cats are most unlikely to hurt a baby intentionally, but cribs and baby

Right: this cat exemplifies the characteristics of his wild ancestors. To many cat lovers it is the restrained hunter within every cat that is part of their appeal. The cat's inscrutable expression also helps to make him appear rather aloof.

Above: although it might seem an unlikely combination to keep birds and a cat — especially if the birds are not caged — many surprising animal relationships can be established if they are introduced at an early age. Nevertheless this combination always carries a risk.

Left: sharp claws and a remarkable sense of balance make cats natural climbers. Practically all cats love a tree to climb, where they can derive a sense of security and are able to survey possible prey from their vantage point.

carriages are nice snug places, and there is always the temptation for them to snuggle up against the baby's face. It's senseless to take needless risks, or to be deprived of the benefit of an affectionate pet, so the simple answer is a cat net when the cat has access to the same room as the baby. And remember, children will derive great pleasure from your pets as they grow up together; they also learn to love and appreciate animals.

A kitten is more likely to adjust happily than a mature cat to children about the house.

There is no reason why a cat should not live happily with other pets either — even dogs and goldfish!

Most of us know of instances where dogs and cats live very amicably together, and it is really only a matter of how they are brought up. The ideal way is for puppy and kitten to grow up together. An adult can sometimes be introduced successfully, but much depends on the individual. The best way to tackle the introductions is discussed on page 20.

Mice, hamsters and birds are almost certain to come off worst in any encounter with a cat. It is best not to put them to the test. Fortunately these animals usually live in cages, so any danger is reduced somewhat. However, it is wise not to tempt a cat where a paw can be squeezed between the bars.

Fish should not present any problems. Cats soon begin to take fish for granted, and a firm 'no' should be quite sufficient to deal with any inquisitiveness. But there's one sure path to peace of mind — an aquarium cover. This is a desirable piece of aquarium equipment anyway.

Choosing a breed

Having decided *whether* to buy a cat, next comes the more tantalizing question of *which* breed. There are so many lovely breeds, not to mention the sometimes charming non-pedigree cats one sees.

No one else can tell you which is the right type of cat for you, but there are

Above: pets should always eat from bowls reserved for their use, and not from dinner plates. A suitable type will be shallow and shaped so that it will not tip easily.

Right: the Siamese is a very vocal breed, and even kittens will make themselves heard when they want attention.

Left: this picture shows the characteristic ear tufts and long whiskers found in most longhaired cats. They have a full-faced expression which can make them look very beguiling. The ruff of hair around the neck should always frame the face.

guidelines which can help to narrow the field.

How important a pedigree is to you will depend on what you are looking for in your pet. If it's pure playful companionship and cat company, or just a family pet with no strong intention of breeding or showing, then you are likely to get just as much pleasure from a cross-bred non-pedigree cat as a pure-bred. Such cats are inexpensive — often free to a good home. And remember, the humble cross-bred cat can make it to the show bench at even the biggest and most prestigeous shows, such as the National Cat Shows in London and New York. Here, alongside the aristocrats of the cat world, there are classes such as 'Rescued cat under two years that was originally a stray' and 'Most appealing expression', or 'Most unusual looking'; so don't feel you'll be debarred totally from the show bench if you are bitten by the exhibition bug.

Inevitably, though, the true aristocrats are the pedigree pure breeds. Unlike a cross-bred kitten you know exactly what he is going to be like when he grows up — visually and to some extent temperamentally. And the years of carefully controlled breeding have emphasized the very best characteristics of the breed.

Naturally, if the thought of exhibiting or breeding seriously appeals to you, then do not hestitate to buy pedigree stock — and the best you can afford.

For some cat lovers the choice of breed is straightforward — they have seen one they've fallen in love with.

For those who have not already made a choice, there are objective ways of narrowing the field.

Deciding whether you should have a longhair or a shorthair is usually fairly easy — if you do not have the time for *regular* (that means *daily*) and thorough grooming, or the thought of long hairs on your furnishings disturbs you, then the choice must be a shorthair.

On the other hand the extra grooming and attention a longhair needs is a price many cat lovers are only to pleased to pay for the privilege of owning these very beautiful cats. Indeed, the regular grooming sessions can be periods of much togetherness and pleasure for cat and owner.

Having narrowed the field in terms of length of hair, it is then largely a matter of deciding which cat appeals to you — and in the choice of breed, as in anything else, beauty is in the eye of the beholder. You will have scores to choose from, and most of them are descibed in this book.

There is no substitute for seeing a breed 'in the flesh' of course, and perhaps the best place to do this is at a cat show. Here you will find examples of all the principal breeds. When you've narrowed the choice to a few breeds, try to see the cats in their home environment. This will also give you a chance to ask any questions that you may still have about the breeds.

You will find both show dates and breeders listed in specialist publications. Your local newsstand will be able to advise you on these. Local newspapers also tend to list breeders with cats for

Right: kittens love something to climb into, and like these two Siamese will sometimes find the most unconventional places to hide.

Far right: be careful when buying a white cat, as those with blue eyes are sometimes incurably deaf. White cats with eyes of other colors, or only one blue eye, usually have perfectly satisfactory hearing. If in doubt, make a sudden noise when the kitten's not looking in your direction.

sale. The classified pages of the local telephone directory may also help.

Cat or kitten?

Most of us start with a kitten and indeed it's a pity to miss those exciting early months. If you wish to exhibit, you are unlikely to be able to buy a good adult pedigree cat cheaply. On the other hand if you are only looking for a household pet it's well worth considering giving a home to a cat from an animal welfare centre. Adult cats often take longer to settle in than a kitten, but some adapt very quickly and become as affectionate as one acquired as a kitten.

Deciding on sex

As both male and female neutered cats are equally well behaved and affectionate, you are only likely to have a strong preference if you intend to show or breed. Otherwise it's just as important to select the brightest and healthiest or the most appealing (provided health is good).

If you're not buying from an expert and you have doubts about the sex of your chosen kitten, look at the genitals. With males these are spaced further from the anus than with females. This will be obvious in a mixed litter, but remember that the male's testicles will probably not have descended.

Where and how to buy

If you will be happy with a non-pedigree cat you should be able to obtain one cheaply — often they are advertised free to good homes. This is fine, but be just as stringent in your selection for health as you would be if you were buying an expensive pedigree cat. The points to look for when buying are described in the next column.

Although a pet store may seem an obvious place to go, be very careful before you buy. You can usually tell if it's a good store by the cleanliness of both store and cages. A good store will also agree to let you return the animal within a few weeks should it become ill. If these conditions are met and the kitten is in good health, there's no reason why you should be disappointed.

Pedigree cats are nearly always bought from breeders of course, and you will find most of them very helpful and knowledgeable. But don't think that because you are dealing with a professional that you don't need to satisfy yourself you are buying a happy and healthy animal.

Don't look at the breeder askance with disbelief if he tells you that the pure white Siamese kitten really will have seal points when it grows up, or that the pale milk chocolate colored kitten really is a Brown Burmese. Some breeds do change colour as they mature, although others, such as Tabbies, are fixed at birth. Do not pay too much attention to eye colour in a young kitten either — they are all blue at birth and will not attain their true color for about 12 weeks.

The moment of truth comes when you have to make the final decision to take one and leave the others. Keep a level head and try to view them all objectively, without being swayed purely by a pathetic or appealing expression.

As kittens should either be playing actively or sleeping, be suspicious of any of them who are sulking quietly at the back of the cage

Examine a kitten by working from head to tail, starting with the nose, which should show no sign of discharge. Nor should there be any soreness round the eyes. Ears can be especially important — watch for sores or parasites or any sign of discharge, especially if he keeps shaking his head or scratching his ears.

Stroke his back, making sure the coat is smooth and silky, with no sign of fleas. Feel the tummy to make sure it is not distended or swollen.

Finally, check the tail end. There should not be any sign of diarrhoea or worms round the anus.

If all's well so far, it's worth checking hearing — especially in white cats with blue eyes, which are sometimes incurably deaf. Rustle a bag, click your fingers or clap your hands when the kitten has its back to you.

Forms and feeding

If you're buying a pedigree cat you'll want a copy of the pedigree certificate — and if you intend to exhibit, ask about transfer of ownership forms.

An equally important document is a certificate of inoculation. This is for feline

infectious enteritis (feline panleucopaenia), a very serious disease (see page 32).

Before you set off home with your kitten ask about its diet. You can set up your own routine once he's settled in, but it is advisable to maintain his established eating habits for the first week or so. He'll have enough adjusting to do besides being faced with totally new foods at unexpected mealtimes.

Your own life will be made easier, too, if you check which cat litter has been used. You can change it in time, but he's more likely to use a brand of litter he knows.

Getting him home

A cat carrier is a very useful acquisition, but if you don't have one when you collect your cat, the supplier will usually have a suitable cardboard carrier you can use. Some old newspapers or rags in the bottom will be satisfactory, and ventilation holes are essential.

It is, however, worth investing in a traveling carrier as you're almost sure to need to take him on a journey again, if only to the vet.

Do make sure your carrier or box is well secured. A cat can escape very quickly, and it isn't much fun chasing him through busy streets. Also it can be dangerous to have a cat loose in the car.

On the way home, talk to him, but don't open the box, even though this is a tremendous temptation. If you're driving alone, the best place for the box is on the floor; otherwise a companion can hold it on his knee. It is wise to take someone with you in case your pet becomes fretful.

Home and dry . . . or is it?

Once home, everyone will want to cuddle and play with him: it's only natural. But it's also overwhelming for your pet. Try to restrain yourselves if that's possible, and although he'll appreciate company and petting, it's important not to overdo it.

Keep your new pet confined to just one room to start with, and give him a chance to explore that before allowing any more freedom. Don't overcrowd him and don't immediately push a bowlful of food under his nose. By the time he's explored round all the chairs and had a look behind the curtains he'll be more relaxed and ready for food. The food you give him will depend largely on what he's been used to eating.

However, from the start a sanitary tray and a bowl of clean water should always be available. Remember to keep his own feeding bowls for his exclusive use — don't be tempted to feed him off your own plates!

Your pet's bed should of course have been thought about in advance and be ready for him. A grocery box will serve quite adquately if nothing better is available, though it must be thrown away when soiled. Wicker baskets are popular, but are difficult to clean and do little to keep out draughts! If you do choose a wicker basket your pet will appreciate one which has a high back and preferably some top cover. Plastic or glass-fibre beds are much the best in terms of ease of cleaning and disinfecting.

Once he seems to be sure of himself gradually allow him to explore other parts of the house, but keep a close watch until

Above: play is vitally important to kittens. Many of their games are really preparation for hunting skills which they will require later. Kittens will play quite happily with everday objects such as cotton reels, screwed up balls of paper, or even clothes pegs . . .

Toys and Games

Like all youngsters, kittens love to play and to be amused, and games form an essential part of their natural development.

You can provide your kitten with two kinds of stimulation — there are those games where you participate, and those he can be left alone with to amuse himself.

Kittens love someone to play with them. They probably chased their mother's tail, which she would have flicked for them, and romped with their litter-mates. It's all part of a game that's really a rehearsal for hunting when the cat is older. You can play the mother's role by using screwed up paper or silver foil tied to a string to pull along. Or you can swing it to and fro as a variation. Action games are the order of the day at playtime. They will keep the kitten amused and he will learn to synchronize his movements.

Self-help toys can be as simple as sheets of crumpled newspapers, an old cardboard box, or a ball of wool (though this isn't a good idea if anyone in the household knits! As with

Above: home is where you make it . . . and cats often have a habit of ignoring the nesting site you've carefully prepared, establishing their own alternative. It's best to try to persuade her to set up home in what you consider to be the most suitable place.

children, it's often the inexpensive toy that is the most enjoyed. A ping-pong ball, being light and easily knocked, is also likely to be appreciated. Small rattle balls on elastic can be hung on something like a door handle, to keep an active kitten happy for many hours.

Most of us tend to succumb to the temptation to buy a toy mouse. Whether your kitten will appreciate a wind-up or still mouse must depend on his personality. The chances are you'll tire of winding up before he tires of chasing.

The range of cat toys at most pet shops is more than sufficient. Some contain dried catnip, which is the catmint of our gardens. Cats love the scent, which really seems to animate them.

Never underestimate the importance of toys and playtime, for it forms an important part of a kitten's development, and if deprived of this stimulation he will make his own amusement by tearing up the best cushion covers or climbing up the curtains.

he can be trusted. Then you can build up to the first short excursion into the garden, rewarding him with a titbit and making a fuss of him.

Your kitten will need lots of attention during the early months. Like young children they need frequent feeding and like to be amused. And because they're still innocent you'll have much the same worries about open fires, hot cooker rings, and so on.

Training and discipline

Claws and instinct can combine to cause damage to chair and table legs if the clawing is not forestalled by providing a scratching post.

If you're a handy sort of person, you can quite easily make a scratching post from an old log that won't splinter, or by gluing a piece of old carpet to a suitable frame. Alternatively, you can buy one from a pet store. You may need to encourage your pet to use it by putting his claws on the post when he decides to try them out elsewhere. Choosing a post with catnip usually encourages the kitten to use it.

Being intelligent creatures, cats are usually quick to learn. Certainly you are unlikely to have much difficulty with toilet training. In fact your pet will possibly have the idea already, having learned from his mother to use a sanitary tray. If he does need a little encouragement, it is usually sufficient to say 'no' and to point to the sanitary tray. You can do a little scratching in the litter to make it clear what you have in mind. Cats very quickly take the point.

Do remember to renew the litter regularly, however, for cats are very fastidious and won't use material that needs changing. Any time spent in this respect will be rewarded with a well-trained pet.

If you intend to use a collar or leash, it is worth getting your kitten used to these. Pet stores usually have a range of collars, but be sure to buy an elastic type so that your pet can free himself if he gets hooked on anything. If your pet is a longhair and you intend to show him it may be advisable to bear in mind that a collar might spoil his ruff.

It's popular to put the pet's name on a disc attached to the collar but this would enable someone to entice him away by calling his name. It is far better to use your own name and phone number.

Before you attempt to attach a leash, let your pet get used to wearing a collar or harness for a few days, but don't leave it on continuously. Once this has been accepted, try attaching the leash, allowing it be dragged around the room (but only do this while you are there to supervise). When this has been accepted you can try holding the other end and following him round the room. Soon you'll be ready to venture on your first excursion. Don't be surprised, however, if your pet stubbornly refuses to budge; another cat might dash round wildly. But with luck you'll eventually be able to persuade him to come *your* way. So much depends on the cat's psychological characteristics. Some breeds, such as Siamese, take more readily than others to this form of training.

Cat doors or flaps enable the cat to come and go as he pleases, and save you the chore of getting up each time he wants to come in or go out. Of course it means he's equally likely to bring his

Far right: Cats and dogs are able to live harmoniously, especially if they are brought up together from the time they were kittens and puppies. They often develop a deep affection for each other.

stray friends home, and it certainly isn't a good idea if you have a female on heat. Try to choose a lightweight flap, counter-balanced so that it doesn't close too rapidly, otherwise he could end up with a rather sore tail!

While training your pet, keep commands simple: just single words such as 'here' or 'come' are best. At mealtimes you may find he begins to know the sound of a tin being opened or a box of something being shaken or opened. These cues will develop naturally.

Don't get too carried away with the training and teach him tricks that may be fine for a kitten but can be quite alarming when performed by an adult cat. A kitten jumping on someone's shoulder or head is one thing, it's quite another with an older cat.

Domestic adjustments

Many people are surprised what a profound effect owning a cat can have on their lives . . . even the plants you grow and the home DIY materials you use can be influenced by our feline friends. Certain poisonous houseplants, such as philodendrons and dieffenbachia will have to be banned — even hydrangeas can be a problem.

Paint strippers and thinners and some disinfectants and detergents will poison a cat even though they are perfectly safe for us to use. It's especially important to realize that solvents such as kerosene or turpentine can be harmful to a cat and can burn his skin; so don't dash for the turps if he gets paint on his coat! Instead, rub off as much of the paint as you can, and then wash the area with soapy water. You can try rubbing a little gin (or rubbing alcohol) into the fur to remove paint.

Obviously with any animal you must be careful with the chemicals you use in the garden. Use only safe insecticides if your cat is likely to brush against or eat leaves, and always place slug pellets out of reach of prying paws.

You may even end up making minor structural alterations to your home. If you have an entire female she'll spend much time and effort trying to get out while on heat. Closing all the doors and windows is not an entirely satisfactory answer in the middle of a hot summer. A framework over the window with plastic-covered netting will provide both ventilation and security.

Introducing Your Cat to Dogs and Children

If you already have a dog in your home it is difficult to know in advance how they are going to react, so it's always advisable to get them used to each other gradually. The kitten will probably be no more than nervous, though the dog may be openly hostile. An adult cat is also likely to be uneasy in this situation. Sometimes, however, the dog will do no more than sniff the new arrival and then ignore him.

Make the introductions in stages. Keep your newcomer in one room, your other pet in another. Then change rooms so that they get used to each other's scent. Then after a couple of days you can try them together — but make sure you are there to supervise! And keep the first encounter brief. This is not to say cats and dogs can't be good friends, but it's only prudent to make sure things get off to a good start. And remember that animals can become jealous just as humans can, so don't fuss the new pet too much in front of the old one. This tip is useful even if it's a second cat you're introducing, for adult cats sometimes resent the intrusion of another cat in the household.

Jealousy in cats can also show itself sometimes if a new baby arrives. If he shows signs of resentment, just give him a little extra attention and soon the whole family will be on the way back to a normal routine.

Young children should be watched, and warned about playing too roughly with a kitten. They should be warned in a realistic but not frightening way about putting animals close to their face, or kissing them. They will probably readily appreciate that the claws are sharp and could do nasty damage to an eye, but there's also the slight, but nevertheless real, risk that some disease could be passed on. Ringworm is one instance of a disease that can be passed from cat to human, and worms are another.

Above: it is in the nature of all kittens to explore whenever they have the opportunity, and climbing is a skill they soon acquire. Cats have a tremendous sense of balance, and of course excellent claws with which to grip and take support.

Above right: it will be apparent to anyone who takes an interest in cats that they are very clean, indeed fastidious, creatures. They constantly preen themselves, and it is only very rarely that a cat needs a bath — perhaps if something has been spilt on his coat.

Left: most people think of cats as being fond of cow's milk, and indeed most cats enjoy it. But with kittens it is wise to watch for signs of diarrhoea which it sometimes causes. The solution is to switch to evaporated milk if this happens.

Feeding your cat

Kittens need food little and often, but by the time your pet is six or seven months old he should be down to just two meals a day. But whatever the age, he will appreciate having the meal served in the same place each time — the kitchen being a fairly practical room. Remember that cats like to pull pieces off the plate and onto the floor, so it's always a good idea to have a suitable rubber mat or newspaper under the dish.

Cats, being creatures of habit, like to have their food served at the same time each day.

The amount served will again depend on age. A kitten of nine weeks will need at least *four* small meals a day. As a guide, a tablespoonful (20ml) should be enough. The meals should consist of two milk-based and two meat-based at this age. The meat can be almost any meat (raw or cooked), although pork and canned meat is probably best avoided at this stage. It is, however, advisable to mince it so that the tiny mouth can cope more easily. Fish is fine, provided you don't feed it every day. Too much fish can lead to health problems. Too much liver can cause loose motions. And cats of all ages appreciate having meals served at room temperature.

Never introduce new foods suddenly to the exclusion of the old favourites, otherwise it may cause digestive problems. Introduce new foods gradually.

Although we all have a mental image of cats lapping a bowl of cow's milk, it does sometimes cause diarrhoea in kittens; if this happens just change to canned milk immediately.

A few drops of cod-liver or halibut oil added to the meat meals won't come amiss for kittens, but they should not be necessary after six months if you are feeding a balanced diet.

A balanced diet for an adult cat should include proteins, fats and carbohydrates, as well as minerals and vitamins. But don't go in for a *Cordon Bleu* menu — they don't have human tastes and plain meals are best.

As the cat is a carnivorous animal he should have fresh meat every day. Meat, apart from pork, can be safely fed raw. Among the meats you can try are hearts from any animal; beef, sheep or chicken liver; beef, lamb or cooked pork kidneys; brains, tripe, spleen: or any of the usual cuts of beef, lamb, sheep, horse or chicken. Steer well clear, however, of cured meat such as ham or any spiced, prepared meat. Fish should be cooked until the flesh comes off the bone easily. Remember to remove the bones.

Even if your pet shows a decided preference for one type of meat, don't feed it to him at every meal. Certain meats can cause problems if fed continuously to the exclusion of all other kinds.

If your cat likes vegetables, they must be cooked first. You will usually find that cats will eat green beans, carrots, strained spinach and tomatoes — but it's worth trying others. Mashed potatoes can also be tried, especially with gravy to add flavour to the meal.

You may, of course, prefer to use ready-prepared foods, and these certainly save time. You can be fairly sure that any reputable make of cat food will be good for your cat, but it's always worth giving your pet other foods as well from time to time. Dry food or cereal is usually appreciated too

If you have difficulty getting your cat in at night, you have a trump card with the evening meal. Don't serve it until you want him in for the night.

Fussy eating habits set in during the early days, so don't give in to your kitten's fads too readily. And if he refuses a particular food, give it a miss for a couple of days then try again.

If he doesn't seem hungry for several meals, he could either be ill or catching his own food in the form of rodents or birds.

What may seem an odd part of your pet's nutritional needs is grass. Not that

Above: the characteristic ruff of fur round the neck and the long hair of the ear tufts can be seen clearly in this longhaired cat.

he needs grass at every meal, but if he has access to grass outdoors he will eat it himself when it's needed. Cats kept indoors should have a supply available for an occasional nibble — either cut or grown in a pot.

Grooming

Grooming is necessary for all cats and essential for longhairs. But grooming is more than just brushing the coat — it gives you an opportunity to inspect teeth and ears as well.

Start grooming from an early age, so that your cat becomes use to it, otherwise you may end up having a struggle.

A stiff brush (bristle for longhairs, rubber for shorthairs) and a metal comb with close teeth are all that's really necessary, though a cloth or glove for smoothing the coat and giving it a nice finish is useful. At times you may have to resort to a pair of blunt-ended scissors if he's managed to find some chewing gum to roll in.

Place the cat on a suitable table covered with newspapers. With a shorthair it is sufficient to comb from head to tail, then brush in the same direction. Firm hand stroking or polishing with the cloth or glove will finish the job nicely and bring a lovely sheen to his coat.

Longhairs are naturally more difficult and here a modicum of patience is required. The first job is to unravel any mats and tangles, which tend to be especially troublesome in the spring and fall. They will need to be teased out, and a knitting pin is quite good for this job. When it comes to combing and brushing, work first from the tail to head, brushing upwards in short strokes, then you can comb in the direction of hair growth. Face, stomach, legs and tail will need just the comb. You should finish with the coat standing away from the body. To make the most of the neck ruff, brush this so that it frames the face.

Sometimes the coat gets to the stage where a bath is the only answer. Although this may seem a good idea to you, your pet probably won't agree, and you should brace yourself for a battle of wills, especially if it's a wet bath.

For a wet bath you would do well to have an assistant — but not the whole family as an audience; it's trying enough for the cat, without spectators. You can use a plastic bowl or the sink; a small non-slip mat such as those sold for baby baths will give your pet more assurance. You'll need a shampoo, but don't use a medicated type. And avoid any that might contain phenol, creosol, chloroxylenol, iodine or iodophor. Have everything to hand, including towels. You

Above: it's not only humans who like to sunbathe. Cats are also notorious sun worshipers, and will often seek out a warm, sheltered spot in which to while away a few hours in the sun.

Right: even when a cat is apparently at rest, such as this lovely Silver Tabby, they are usually alert to any activity, and ready to spring into action almost without warning.

might also like to smear petroleum jelly or eye ointment round the eyes to act as a barrier to prevent soap reaching them. Cotton in the ears will prevent water entering and causing distress.

Three or four inches of water should be sufficient, and it should be no warmer than 27°C (80°F). Place him gently in the water, talking all the time, and stroking. Then using a jug, pour water over his back, working slowly and gently. If he reacts violently to this, and the water is no more than hand hot, it may be best to adopt another approach and wrap a soaked towel round him leaving head out, of course, to wet the fur. Once the coat is wet you can rub in the shampoo, being careful to avoid eyes, nose and mouth. Allow a few minutes for the shampoo to take effect, but talk to your pet to keep him reassured, then once you have worked up a good lather he can be rinsed. It should not be necessary to apply any further shampoo.

A brisk rub down with towels will soon get the surplus water off him, but he should not be allowed outside for a few hours. Ideally all this should be done on a warm sunny day, but this is not always possible. Some cats enjoy a hair drier used on them, but be very gentle on him if it's used, and don't use it if the cat shows signs of distress.

Sometimes a cat doesn't need an all-over bath, the tail end and feet being the only parts in really urgent need of a good clean.

You may find that the bath has loosened hairs, so once the fur is dry, comb out any loose hair and groom.

Cats with a dark coloured coat are sometimes given a bran bath, especially if being exhibited. The bran, which is obtainable from pet stores, should be heated in the oven for half an hour at 300°F. With newspaper laid out first, the bran is worked thoroughly into the fur. This is usually a pleasurable experience for the cat. The bran is then brushed out, but it must be done thoroughly, especially if you are about to exhibit the cat.

It is inevitable that the cat will shed hairs naturally, but it is usually more of a problem in the spring. A number of factors are responsible, including temperature, humidity, condition of skin, and day length. Day length is obviously more of a factor with wild cats and those which live permanently outdoors than it is with indoor cats, where artificial light confuses the situation.

The answer to loose hairs on furniture and clothes is to be sure you comb and groom the coat *every* day.

Left: this thoughtful-looking Tabby kitten is just seven weeks old. By this stage he should be practically weaned and almost ready to leave his mother, although it is best to wait until about ten weeks before taking kittens away.

Above: the Abyssinian is a very attractive cat of 'foreign' appearance. This is a Red Abyssinian, and it clearly shows the very distinctive coat of these cats. Each hair is ticked with bands of a darker color, creating a most subtle shade.

Chapter

2 Health and Pregnan

y

A neurotic owner, constantly watching and waiting for one ill or another to befall his cat, is not going to do his pet much good. If anyone worried about all the diseases to which they *might* succumb, nobody would keep pets. Most of the problems described in this chapter will never present themselves. If you're lucky none of them will.

There are some problems you must expect to crop up at some time or other — such as fleas and worms. But they're easily controlled and there is no need to banish your pets because of them.

Some symptoms will present themselves without you having to look for them, but grooming time gives you an opportunity to watch for ear, eye and skin troubles, not to mention fleas. It's also an opportunity to inspect feet.

The importance of knowing something about common ailments lies in the fact that you can then spot problems quickly and take the appropriate action. Often ailments are much more easily controlled if remedial action is taken quickly. But remember, reading about symptoms should not turn you into a do-it-yourself vet! There is no substitute for professional advice.

Left: a healthy cat is a happy cat, and this alert pet looks fit. Many health problems can be overcome easily if identified and treated in the early stages.

Left: kittens will soon start to explore, and it does not take long before they have their first tree adventures. Because they do not have such perfect balance at this stage, and are sometimes unwilling to jump down, it is wise to be available to provide a helping hand.

Far left: cats of all ages love to hide among flowers, and this Seal Point Siamese is no exception.

Vaccination

Just as a thoughtful and considerate mother will have her children vaccinated against certain diseases which could prove serious or fatal, so a wise cat owner will make sure his pet is protected. Vaccinations are not possible for all diseases, and the degree and length of immunity varies in certain instances, but your vet will always advise you. If you wish to exhibit your cat, or take it to a cattery during vacation, or to stud, then you will probably find it won't be accepted without evidence of certain injections.

The one you must not miss is that for feline infectious enteritis, as it is known in Britain — feline panleucopaenia in America. This unpleasant disease is described in the following pages. It used to be a dreaded illness, usually resulting in death. If you have your pet vaccinated, you can relax. The first injection should be given at about two to three months of age, and it may have had this before you receive the kitten (you'll expect to have a certifcate to that effect from the supplier). The certificate will also tell you the type of vaccine used, and your vet will be able to advise you when booster doses are necessary.

Cat flu is another name for feline viral rhinotracheitis. Vaccines against this and a very similar disease known as feline picornavirus infection (which also gets labelled as cat flu), are available, though protection tends to be short-lived. The degree of protection afforded is complicated for the same reason that it is difficult to produce a cold vaccination for humans — there are so many different strains that cause the symptoms. These diseases are usually known as pneumonitis in the United States of America.

Rabies, thankfully, at the present, is practically unknown in Britain, but that's not so in other countries. Your vet will advise you on vaccination, and you'll certainly need to have your pet treated if you want to travel abroad with him.

Some common ailments

There is always the danger of reading through a list of ailments and reaching the conclusion that owning a cat must be one continual worry, with a regular place in the line at the vet's. But cats are hardy creatures, and provided you have your pet vaccinated you are unlikely to be troubled by anything much more serious than fleas. Nevertheless, having an idea of what might be wrong can often result in prompt preventive action. But remember, it is no substitute for a vet's professional advice.

Abscesses show themselves as hard, shining swellings. Your pet will also look thoroughly miserable, and probably resent handling. The temperature is usually raised. If the abscess is in the ear he will hold his head on one side and there may be a thick greenish yellow discharge. Cats suckling kittens sometimes develop a breast abscess, and it will be clear that it is causing her pain.

If the abscess is in the ear or breast then leave it to your vet to treat with antibiotics. On other sites hot fomentations applied every couple of hours may help. But consult your vet if possible; he may decide to lance it.

Alopecia reveals itself as bald patches, sometimes quite large. Fortunately the disease is not contagious and your vet will probably prescibe hormone treatment.

Bladder stones are usually revealed when you see your pet trying to pass urine but only managing a few drops, and even that with a plaintive cry. The bladder may be obviously distended and painful. Don't waste any time in getting him to the vet. The problem is more common in males.

Bites should always be treated. What looks like a small surface wound may be quite deep. Apply a hot fomentation about every five hours, so that the wound heals slowly but cleanly, allowing pus to drain away.

Bronchitis is more troublesome with older cats, particularly if they are overweight. Rapid breathing, panting and possibly a wheezy cough are the main symptoms. But remember these could be the onset of cat flu or some other serious illness. It's always worth checking with your vet as he will prescribe suitable medicines. You will have to keep the animal warm but with adequate ventilation. Keep the meals small and light, and try him on warm milk.

Cat flu can affect any cat, but some breeds such as Abyssinian, Burmese and Siamese, seem to be ready victims to it. The first symptoms are a catarrhal nasal discharge and sneezing, with a temperature above normal that may rise to 40°C (104°F).

The cat may also dribble, and a watery discharge from eyes and nose will turn yellow and sticky after a few days, eyelids becoming puffy and swollen. Vomiting and dehydration may follow. There is no cure, so it is really a matter of treating the symptoms, which is best left to the vet.

Do not take your pet to him without

Right: this picture of contentment is just one week old, yet already he is showing an interest in life. It is best to avoid the temptation to handle them too much at this stage.

Far right: Siamese kittens are usually all white, but this queen has obviously been sired by a male of another breed. The result is a litter of half-bred kittens, but none the less charming for that.

phoning first if you suspect cat flu (he may want to visit you at home).

Some protection is available from vaccinations, and you can be reassured that the disease cannot be transmitted to humans.

Claws are important to a cat and they do need clipping from time to time. It's best for the cat and best for you and your soft furnishings as front claws that are too long tend to be destructive.

It's normally only the front claws that need clipping. Use special clippers, which you can buy from a good pet shop, and get someone to hold your pet while you do the actual clipping. A little pressure on the pads will encourage the claws to come from their sheaths. Cut at right angles to the claw, being very careful not to cut into the quick (the pink part).

Some people have their cat declawed, but it is not to be recommended, and any cat that has been treated this way is barred from shows in Britain.

Cystitis is inflammation of the bladder, and shows itself as a frequent desire to urinate, but only being able pass small amounts. Appetite will decrease and temperature increase. It should clear up satisfactorily with antibiotics prescribed by your vet.

Dermatitis is an inflammation of the skin, and can be due to a variety of causes. Your vet will help to discover the cause and also give you a suitable ointment.

Ears are prone to a number of troubles, including parasites, excessive wax, and dirt.

You will need a flash light to investigate properly. Wax is dealt with quite simply by using three or four drops of warmed glycerine or olive oil from a dropper. After waiting a few minutes you should be able to remove the wax with cotton swabs. More than one application may be needed. But be careful as cats' ears are very sensitive and you must be careful not to probe too deeply. Always treat ears as the delicate instruments they are.

A cheesy-smelling waxy secretion that tends to dry into scabs at the entrance to the ear could mean otorrhoea (canker). Close examination could reveal ulceration. Don't try home treatment, see a vet.

Very tiny reddish-brown mites are probably ear mange mites. Again it's best to let the vet prescribe a treatment, though in the meantime you can be softening any wax as described above.

A reddening in the ear accompanied by a thin yellowish discharge could be otitis (inflammation). Once again your vet will prescribe treatment.

All the ear troubles described are accompanied by a flicking or twitching of the ears or head, and the cat frequently tries to scratch the ear.

When doing anything to a cat's ears it is worth wrapping him in a special cat bag.

Eczema is another problem that can be caused by various situations. Your vet should be able to help you sort out the cause of your pet's eczema. Wet eczema can be very irritating and results in the cat tending to rub the fur off leaving a patch of moist red skin. Dry eczema looks like small red hives; these often follow the line of a superficial blood vessel. These spots then tend to become infected and merge into each other to form large red patches, from which their hair falls. Warmth makes the irritation worse and the cat will often jump up suddenly and scratch vigorously, and it may lick the areas intensively. Fish used to be thought the cause, but it could be due to a hormone imbalance. Let your vet decide cause and treatment.

Eye troubles are, fortunately, fairly uncommon. Conjunctivitis is the most likely problem you'll come across. An affected eye usually has a blue or milky-white covering. There is often a watery discharge and the animal tends to rub the affected eye. Your vet will prescribe an antibiotic treatment. He's also the person to see if your pet has a piece of foreign matter in the eye if it looks difficult to remove.

Feline infectious enteritis (panleucopaenia) is a very severe disease. Before the days of vaccinations it was the dread of cat owners. Vomiting is usually the first symptom, and there may be diarrhoea. The cat's temperature will be raised in the range of 39-41°C (102-105°F). A significant indication of this is if your pet keeps going to his water bowl (although he'll move only with reluctance) and sits over it unable to drink. Dehydration can result.

There is only one thing to do — call the vet without delay.

Fleas are pretty well known and don't require a detailed description, but it is important to differentiate between flea eggs — which are creamy-white small spheres — and flea dirt, which is gray-black.

Don't be tempted to use DDT. A flea powder based on pyrethrum or derris is

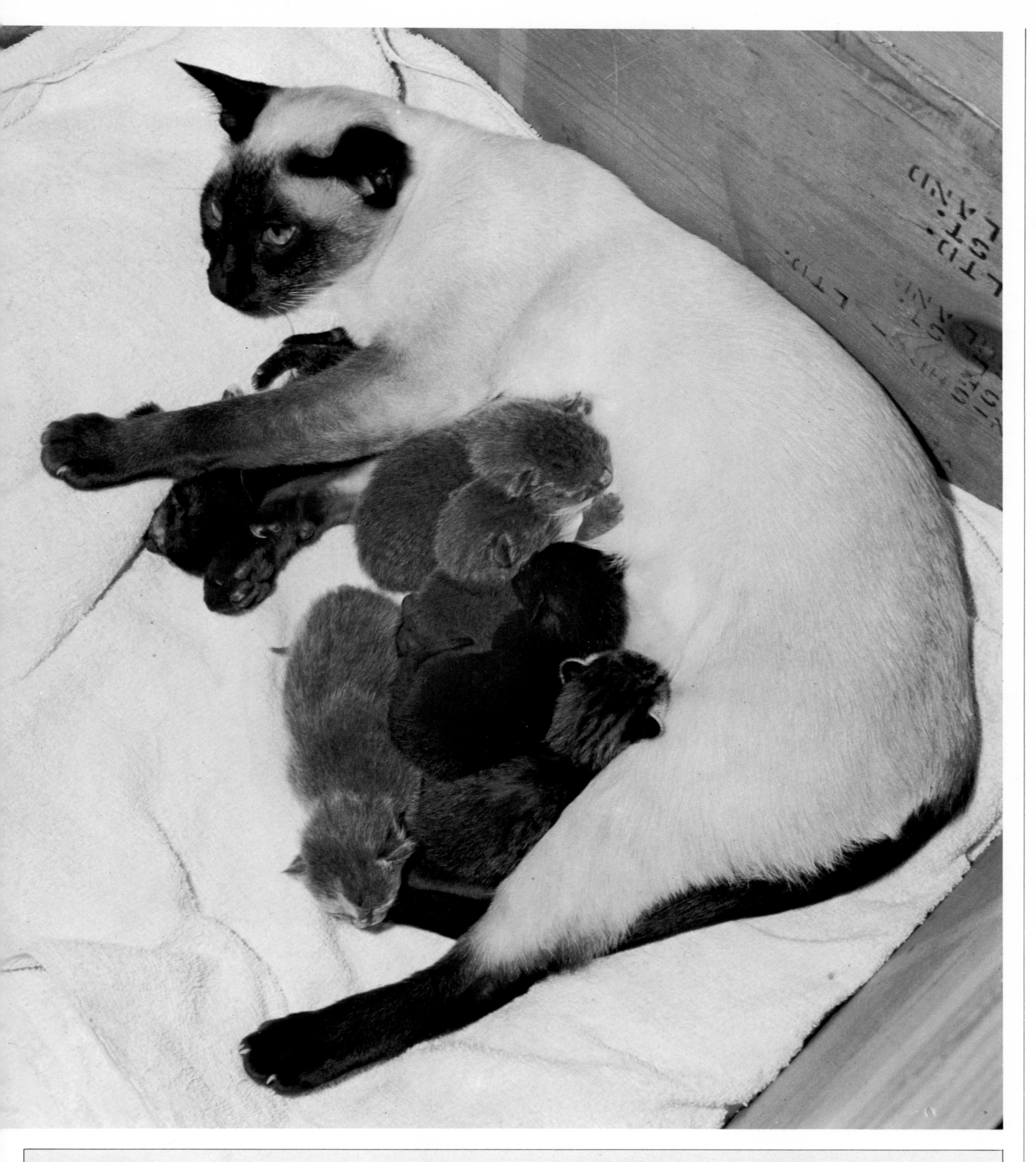

Fur Balls

Cats are always cleaning themselves, so it's not surprising that they swallow hairs. These are usually regurgitated as pellets of matted hair, but sometimes this doesn't work, especially during a moult, and the fur forms a hard ball within the animal.

Symptoms depend on where the ball is sited. Sickness may be evident if it's in the stomach, and the ball may be bought up. Constipation is the natural result of a fur ball in the bowel. In both cases the cat will appear to be hungry for food, but unable to eat when presented with it.

Liberal quantities of veterinary laxative may remove the problem, otherwise your vet will have to be consulted. Prevention is a much better solution, and this is simply a matter of regular grooming. Not surprisingly, fur balls are much more common in longhaired breeds.

Above: Persian kittens always look appealing and there is seldom any difficulty in finding new homes for them. Because they are so endearing it is wise to make potential owners aware of the practical aspects of keeping a longhaired cat.

Preparing for Kittens

Your pet may indicate where she would like to have her kittens by trying to make a nest. A corner of the kitchen or garage, or a large cupboard which has been cleared out may be suitable.

A large box lined with newspapers and an old blanket will be adequate. It's a good idea to have a sanitary tray close by so that she doesn't have too far to go once the kittens arrive.

Of course it's no use making all these preparations if you don't take the precaution of confining her to the house for a few days before the kittens are due. If allowed to go into the garden she may decide to have them outside.

Before the due date it may be worth letting your vet give her the once-over to see whether any difficulties are foreseen. Be reassured, however, that most cats manage perfectly well.

Just to be on the safe side, it's best to have a few things to hand, such as a hot-water bottle and a blanket to wrap it in, and another box or basket lined with newspaper to put the kitten in if you need to while the mother is still giving birth. The only other things you are likely to need are a few clean (boiled) pieces of old towelling, a sheet of polythene to put under the box, and some old newspapers.

Left: cats love to feel a sense of security while they sleep, and the ideal cat bed will be built up at the sides to form a hood over the top. This Persian seems happy with his basket.

usually suitable. Treatments come as powders or aerosols but follow the instructions. And remember that fleas may be on the bedding and elsewhere. Also they are not averse to a meal on man, even though they much prefer cats.

Fur balls, see page 33.

Lice look like cigarette ash to the naked eye, although if you look carefully you'll see they move. Face, neck and armpits are favourite sites for them to appear. The eggs are capsule-shaped.

If you groom regularly lice should never become established, but if they do appear the chances are the flea treatment you use will also control the lice.

Mange is caused by small mites that bore into the skin. There are two kinds. Sarcoptic mange or scab normally affects the area around the ears and head, the skin becoming thickened and inflamed, though other areas can be affected. Because of scratching, secondary infections sometimes set in. The hair falls out to reveal gray, furrowed, skin, which sometimes looks sweaty. There may be a 'mousy' smell. Crusts often form, and these tend to bleed if cracked.

You will be given medication by the vet, but you must isolate your pet as it is contagious — very much so to cats, and to a lesser extent to man. Demodectic mange is less contagious, and with this the scabs are not so extensive. The skin color will be a red tone rather than gray.

Rhumatism can be suspected if your pet walks stiffly and resents being handled. Warmth usually helps, so try a hot water bottle in cold weather. Your vet may suggest a pain killer.

Ringworm is sometimes called fur fungus. In fact three fungi can cause the problem. The symptoms are split and curled hairs, which are later shed to reveal round goose bumps. The cat will be scratching violently, and this causes scabs and a grayish crust to form Bare spots and broken fur are fairly common symptoms. Head and neck are the areas most commonly affected. Ringworm will respond well to treatment prescribed by your vet, but you must follow strict hygiene rules. It is contagious, not only to other cats but humans too, especially children. Wear suitable cotton or rubber gloves when handling the animal and make sure they are boiled or sterilized afterwards. Use newspapers for the cat's bedding and burn them daily.

Worms may sound dreadful but they can be controlled quite easily with worming preparations. There are several types: the round worm 100 mm (4 in) long, although they are usually coiled when you see them; tape worms look very much like pieces of dirty white tape with a serrated edge, though the head end is narrower (segments may break off and look like grains of rice round the anus); hookworms are thin and almost microscopic parasites that are generally more prevalent in hotter parts of the world (this is not the same as the human hookworm). Suitable preparations are available, but if in any doubt consult your vet.

Having kittens

Kittens are so appealing that many cat owners feel they would like to let their pet have at least one litter before having it neutered. But this should only be done if you are prepared to find the kittens good homes.

It is best not to attempt to keep your own entire tom unless you are really going in for breeding in a big way. Entire toms are not suitable for keeping indoors. When they become sexually mature instinct causes them to mark their territory by spraying it with urine. If he happens to regard your lounge as his territory, then he won't hesitate to spray over your furniture and carpets.

So it's a matter of taking your pet to a stud. Of course if you are satisfied with cross-breds, your pet will have no difficulty in finding the local toms. In fact if you don't keep the female indoors during her season she'll be pregnant before you realize it. Even if you keep her indoors, the house will be under siege, with the queen (the name for an entire female cat) desperately trying to get out, and all the neighborhood toms trying to get in.

If you don't want to breed from her at first, there are hormone tablets that will prevent her coming on heat.

It's as well to be prepared for your pet's first heat. This may occur between six and nine months, rarely much earlier, sometimes a little later, especially with Persians.

The first indication you have that a queen is coming into season is usually her rather strange behaviour. No matter how affectionate she's been before, the chances are she'll be even more so now, incessantly rubbing herself against your legs . . . or chair and table legs. She will roll on the floor, and will sometimes

shiver or convulse rhythmically. If you stroke her she may crouch with her bottom up and tail in the air.

She'll also voice her feelings. It is the crying noises that give rise to the term 'calling', which means she's ready for mating. There is a tendency to make treading movements with the back legs when calling like this.

The frequency with which cats come into season varies with both breed and individuals. Twice a year in spring and summer or fall is fairly normal, but some, especially some of the Orientals, seem to their owners either to be on heat, pregnant or nursing.

The length of the heat may last for a few days or a few weeks, sometimes coming on again a few weeks later. There is no exact cycle.

It's not wise to let your pet mate on the first call; wait until she's six months old (or her second call, whichever is the longer) if she's a short-hair Oriental breed. It's best to wait for 12 months or the second heat for a Persian type.

If you want to go in for pedigree stock, and decide to send your pet away to a stud, it's worth joining a cat club and seeking advice about a suitable mate. It's helpful to join a local club anyway: there are general cat clubs and specialist breed clubs, but both should be able to advise you about the location of suitable stud cats.

Make arrangements well in advance, confirming arrangements by phone when you know your pet is ready. It's then normal to take your queen to the tom (the stud owner will advise when you should take her). Don't be surprised if you are asked to pay cash in advance, and don't be upset if you are asked to produce an injection certificate. It is the sign of a considerate breeder. Be prepared to leave your pet for a few days.

When you bring her home from the mating she will usually have stopped calling, but make sure you don't let her out — it is possible for her to mate again with another tom, and you'll have the kitten you were expecting and perhaps some you weren't.

The first sign of pregnancy is when the nipples change to a redder color, from about the 16th day; later they become stiffer and more enlarged. She may later start to roll again, but without calling. It will be about six weeks before there are plainly visible signs of swelling.

Most pregnancies last between 63 and 65 days, but it is not unusual for them to last a few days either side of this number.

The onset of labor is usually indicated by your pet becoming restless, showing little interest in food. She may also keep going to the sanitary tray and looking troubled. Her nest may be rearranged.

Soon you will be able to see the muscles tightening and signs of straining, and you can look forward to the first of several kittens. When they are born they may be enclosed in a membrane, containing the kitten surrounded by fluid.

The cat normally bites through this quickly to release the kitten. If she doesn't show any sign of doing so, you may have to do it for her, using clean finger nails or blunt-ended scissors. Whether the amniotic sac comes with the kitten or follows it, your pet will instinctively bite through the cord about 50 mm (2 in) from the kitten. The placenta follows shortly, and this is the part that can be disturbing if you're not prepared for it — the cat usually eats it. It may seem unpleasant to you, but it is quite natural as it triggers off a hormone reaction which is beneficial to her. She may not eat them all.

It's fairly reasonable to expect four kittens, but be prepared for anything from one to ten.

Kittens are born blind, and most won't open their eyes until they are about nine days old. Watch the cord for the first week and if it shows any signs of inflammation, talk to your vet.

It's also as well to keep an eye on the mother's breasts and to seek help if there is any sign of trouble with suckling. She will also appreciate plenty of milk.

By the fourth week the kittens will be ready to explore the outside world, and they might be showing interest in their mother's bowl of milk.

Above: at this stage, especially when only one kitten remains, it is natural to wish that mother and daughter could remain as close as this. But all too soon the kitten will want independence and mother will show less interest in her offspring.

Left: this Blue Point Siamese has a one-week-old cross-bred kitten. Because the Siamese characteristics are genetically recessive, first-cross kittens never have the Siamese coloring.

Neutering

The world is full of unwanted kittens, so unless you intend to breed responsibly and with serious intentions, it is only fair to have your pet neutered. It may sound drastic and even traumatic for the cat, but it isn't. Cats cope well with these operations and go on to lead extremley contented lives.

Males are castrated — a simple and speedy operation carried out under a general anaesthetic. It can be done at any age, but is always best before the cat reaches sexual maturity. If done afterwards he may have acquired the habit of spraying urine around the the home. The operation is not normally done before 12 weeks, four or five months being the more usual age.

Females have their ovaries and uterus removed — called spaying — which although a more complicated operation is nevertheless a safe one that seems to cause little distress. Recovery is usually rapid. Some vets prefer to perform the operation from the age of ten weeks, but four to five months is more common. Adult cats can, of course, be spayed.

Chapter

3 Cats from the Orien

Cats from the Orient . . . the phrase has romantic and mysterious connotations. And they are indeed cats with mysteries — for the true origins of most of them have been lost in the mists of history, and as a result many romantic legends have developed around these charming creatures.

The cats we usually associate with the Orient — the Siamese, Burmese and the Korat — are all highly distinctive in appearance, with 'foreign' build, and very definite personalities.

Oriental cats are highly intelligent and very affectionate, and perhaps the most dog-like in character. In short, they make very good house pets, and are a good choice if you want a cat that will give you unstinting companionship, and demand much love and attention in return.

Not everyone wishes to teach tricks to their cats, but the Oriental breeds are especially receptive to training. The Siamese and Korat, for instance, will take to a lead quite happily, while retrieving is another speciality. And if it's a question of learning how to open a door latch, then the Siamese won't be slow to learn.

Some of the Orientals will try to hold a conversation, being vocal animals. This is the one major drawback with an entire Siamese queen — when she's on heat the whole neighbourhood will know (it's been known for them to lose their voices as a result!) But not all Orientals have this drawback: the Burmese, for example, has a much quieter voice.

All the Orientals have desirable characteristics, and whichever breed is chosen you are almost certain to be captivated by its charms.

Left: Seal Point Siamese are the most popular of the Oriental breeds, and these three kittens show why. The 'points' are the face mask, ears, feet and tail, which in this case are a nice seal brown.

Above and right: the two cats here are Seal Point Siamese, the basic color for these Oriental cats. The 'points' refer to face mask, ears, legs, feet and tail, which, in the Seal Point, should be a rich seal-brown. The Chocolate Point was an early variation, and breeding has since produced 'points' in a range of colors from Red to Tabby, but all have the same unique disposition and temperament.

Siamese

Siamese cats are usually recognized and admired wherever they go, even by people who know practically nothing about cats. They are certainly distinctive, with lots of visual appeal and charm, and an aristocratic and mystical look about them. In addition they have magnificent poise.

Anyone who hasn't owned a Siamese may not appreciate their capacity for affection and their intelligence. They are very attentive cats, taking an active interest in all that goes on, and fully participating in family life. Many people say they are 'one man' cats, but it's really a matter of upbringing, and if raised in a family atmosphere they will make themselves equally at home with anyone who'll spend time with them. In fact for sheer companionship they are practically unsurpassed. In many ways they are the most dog-like of cats and need human company.

If you give a Siamese love and warmth, it will amply reward you by returning your affection. Equally they can be quite hurt if you neglect them. Being sociable creatures they will even welcome the company of other cats, particularly if you have to leave them during the day, whereas most other cats tend to be solitary by nature except when the mating instinct overcomes them. They are a good

Above and left: Blue Point Siamese — a breed which was first mentioned in 1894, although it is not clear whether such cats were the result of cross-breeding or just a chance mutation. They were certainly being exhibited in both Britain and America by the 1920s. They have the reputation of being less temperamental than Seal Points.

choice if you want a cat to share a home with other pets.

Anyone who has owned a Siamese will tell you stories of their intelligence. They quickly learn how to open suitable latches and will beg for food without much encouragement. And if you start training sufficiently young you should experience no difficulty in persuading your Siamese to walk on a leash.

In short they have an appealing nature; and they are just as appealing and pleasing to look at.

Over the years some quite striking new patternings have been developed, though in the United States of America they have called some of them Shorthair Colorpoints. These include Tortie Point Siamese (Tortie Colorpoint Shorthair), and the fascinating Tabby Point Siamese (Tabby Colorpoint Shorthair).

There are more than eight varieties of Siamese available, with the chance of others being officially recognized all the time. The basic type, and probably the most popular one, is the Seal Point, with its seal-brown face mask, ears, tail, legs and feet over a base color of cream shading to pale fawn on the back. The head has an Oriental look — long and well proportioned, with large well-pricked ears which are wide at the base, narrowing to a pointed tip. The deep clear blue, almost almond-shaped eyes — which are a feature of this cat — should be spaced well apart, having an Oriental, and slanting shape. The body is long and sleek, the legs slim with small oval feet. The long tail should taper to a fine point. Whether it's straight or slightly kinked is a matter of fashion and regional taste. Early Siamese always had a kink in the tail, but today's breeders regard it as a fault, though in Britain a slight kink is still permitted on the show bench if it can only be felt rather than seen.

In fact the first Siamese bred in Britain were in several respects quite different from those we know today. The eyes, for instance, often had a definite squint, yet this is regarded as a fault today. They were also heavier in build and the heads

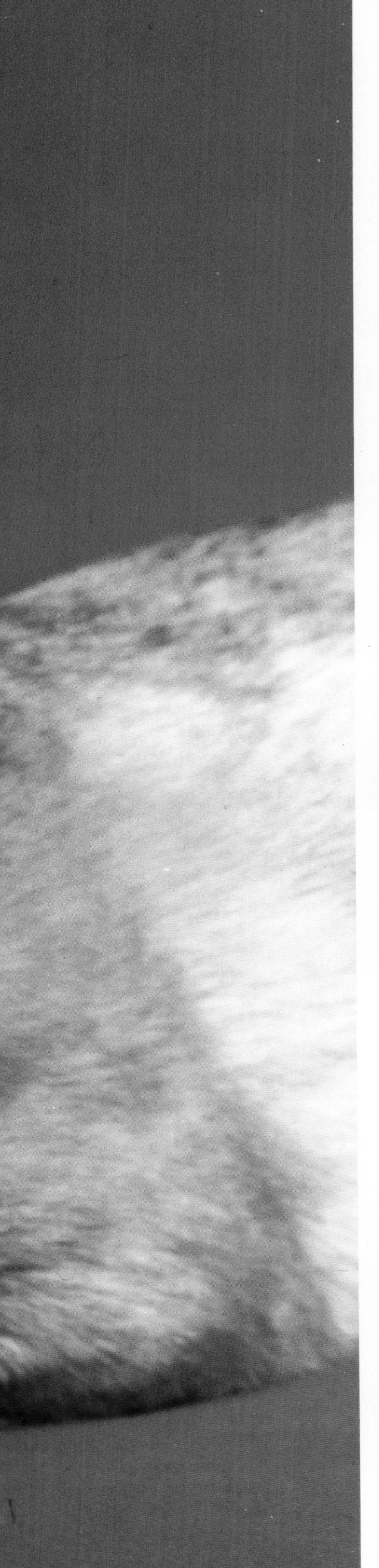

were rounder: more like the British Shorthairs. Today we expect a wedge-shaped head, having a smooth outline from both frontal and profile views.

If the early breeders could see today's Siamese they would be astounded at the hardiness of today's cats. They were once regarded as delicate cats, to be pampered and protected. Whether the breed has become hardier or the over-pampering was born of ignorance is difficult to say, but we know they are hardy animals. It is only during the first few months of life that extra warmth and protection are needed.

Although we have a clear idea of the development of the modern Siamese cat, the true origins of the breed are a little more obscure. Most experts believe the cat has its origins in the East.

It is, perhaps, because of its uncertain history, and appearance of great breeding, that a number of wonderful legends have developed around the Siamese. In fact there are stories to account for most of its physical characteristics.

The lovely blue eyes are supposed to reflect heaven as a reward for a job well done guarding the Buddhist temples.

The squint, which was once regarded as a desirable quality and sign of a true Siamese, has now almost been bred out as an undesirable characteristic. But the story goes that two Siamese cats went into the jungle to search for a royal goblet which had disappeared from one of the temples. After much searching they found the treasure, but feeling it was unsafe to leave the treasure unattended while they went back for the priest, it was agreed that one of them (the male) would go back to the city to tell the priest of their discovery, while his companion remained behind to guard the goblet.

The journey back to the city took many days. Meanwhile the remaining cat would not let the treasure out of her sight, her gaze fixed permanently on the goblet. In fact she stared at it for so long that she began to squint. Eventually she had to sleep, but she curled her tail around the stem of the goblet so that she would awaken if anyone tried to steal it. By the time her companion returned with the priest, she had given birth to five kittens — and all of them had squints and kinked tails.

Another lovely story about the kinked tail tells of a princess in Siam who used to hang her rings on her cat's tail while she went bathing. Once, however, when she returned to put the rings back they had slipped off the cat's tail and were lost. In order to prevent this happening again,

Left: the Tortie Point Siamese is an unusual-looking cat with blotched points. Some American authorities do not regard it as a true Siamese and call it a Tortie Colorpoint Shorthair. This is an all-female breed.

Above: the Lilac Point Siamese is a pleasant-looking cat with pinkish-gray points. It occurs when both parents carry the genes for both Chocolate and Blue. The breed is sometimes known as the Frost Point.

Above: a most striking cat, the Tabby Point Siamese has generated a variety of names. In America it is also known as the Lynx Point Siamese or Colorpoint Shorthair. The legs and tail are especially attractive with their Tabby rings.

Right: the Red Point Siamese, or Red Colorpoint Shorthair as it is sometimes known in America. It is a beautiful cat and quite distinctive.

the next time she tied a knot in her cat's tail, and ever since all Siamese cats have had a kinked tail.

We have some idea of how the cat came to Britain, though experts cannot be absolutely certain. It is thought that the Siamese was introduced into Britain in the 1870s, though it is possible that they first appeared as one of the gifts from the King of Siam to Owen Gould, the British Consul General in Bangkok, in 1884. His sister apparently bred from them and became one of the founder members of the Siamese Cat Club in Britain (there are now specialist clubs in other countries too). There are, however, some who question whether the King of Siam gave these cats to Mr. Gould.

Since then the breed has gone from strength to strength, and anyone who has owned a Siamese will tell you what a wonderful pet they make. The only drawback is their penetrating voice, especially when calling. While not all females will howl, most will create a disturbance which is likely to have your neighbors wondering whether you are ill-treating either your cat or your child. For this reason you may be tempted to consider whether to have her neutered. The noises are sometimes bloodcurdling, and are often made in the middle of the night. Some Siamese have been known to lose their voice through calling.

Siamese seem to come into season at a particularly early age. It is not unusual for them to come on heat by the age of six months, though it is best not to breed from them so early.

If you decide to breed from her, don't be surprised to see an all-white litter. This is quite normal, as the markings don't begin to show until the kittens are a week or two old. It has been known for the ill-informed to be horrified at the sight, thinking their pet's been mated by some unknown father. If there is mixed Siamese parentage, you will be kept in suspense for a while before seeing what varieties you have. The fine marks between the mask and the ears may not be completely defined until the cat is nearly adult.

The kittens tend to be very active and playful, and you may have to impose some discipline quite early if they are not to climb curtains and cause other damage. Compared with other cats, they tend to be advanced for their age and very inquisitive — they'll soon be out of their box and away if you don't watch them.

Siamese make excellent pets, being bright and intelligent, quick to learn tricks and showing real warmth towards their owners. However they are restless by nature and always like to be active and doing things with you. Unlike most cats, they will actually enjoy travelling with you

— but they will fret somewhat if left alone for long periods. So if you are out a lot during the day, it is well worth considering a second cat as a companion.

There is a long-haired Siamese, but as the purists did not take kindly to the thought of a Siamese with long hair, which was considered to spoil the traditional Oriental look of the breed, they were given a new name — Balinese. These are discussed on page 92.

Havana Brown

The Havana Brown has nothing to do with Havana, and during the early days of the breed the British authorities refused to recognize it under that name lest it lead to confusion, so it was called the Chestnut Brown (Foreign) Shorthair. However, the breed, which is of British origin, was exported to the United States of America in 1956 and it was there that the name Havana Brown was established. A few years later Britain had to concede that the new name had become accepted.

The breed was developed from the Chocolate Point Siamese, and in fact crosses are still made back to the Chocolate Point to keep the breed healthy and maintain a dark coat. If you compare the two animals, the very strong Siamese influence will clearly be seen. It is effectively a Siamese without the normal body color. The mahogany-brown fur is, however, a little longer than normal Siamese, though it does lose its color slightly during hot weather, especially the tip of the tail which becomes bleached and develops an almost gingery color. It is obviously best not to show them at this time of year.

Their build is much like the Siamese, as one would expect, with a long head, large pricked ears, svelt body, lithe legs and long, tapering tail. Paw pads are pink.

The eyes, which are blue at birth should turn green within six months; they should be slanting and Oriental in appearance according to the British requirement, though the American standard demands a less 'foreign' appearance and more oval eyes, together with slightly rounded tips to the ears. In the American cat there should also be a more definite 'stop' at the eyes when the head is viewed in profile.

Havana kittens are born with the same dark color as their parents, unlike some other breeds which tend to change.

The Havana makes an ideal pet, being gentle and intelligent and yet very playful. Its voice tends to be quiter than that of the Siamese. It's quite an extrovert, enter-

Left: the Havana looks almost like a Brown Burmese, but the eyes are a definite green and the coat a richer brown. It is in effect a Chocolate Siamese in an all-over color, and to maintain quality they are sometimes crossed back to Chocolate Points.

Above: Cream Burmese are lovely cats, the coat being a rich cream, slightly darker on the face and back, paler on the underparts. Slight Tabby markings are sometimes present, although these should not be too pronounced. Nose leather and foot pads are pink.

taining and a very affectionate breed.

It is best not to subject the Havana to too much cold and damp, which they seem to resent.

Burmese

The Burmese is a delightful breed. It has an extrovert and affectionate nature, more placid than the Siamese which claim a place in its ancestry. It is also less vocal, and not as highly strung as the Siamese. But in common with the Siamese they are intelligent cats, take well to traveling, and will walk on a leash.

Although the breed almost certainly originated in the Burma region, where they were probably the result of a natural mating of a Siamese and an unknown breed with a dark coat, the Burmese is not common in Burma. Its popularity today is due to the early breeding which took place in America, where the breed became recognized in the mid 1930s. After the Second World War the Burmese made its way across the Atlantic. Since then it has made much progress and gained in popularity. There are now many color variations, all of which have the same charming personality.

The main type is the Brown Burmese. At first glance it is not unlike the Havana Brown, though the foot pads, like the nose leather, should be brown, whereas the Havana has pink paw pads. The color should be an all-over dark seal-brown, though it may shade just a little paler on the chest and belly. There is sometimes a slight darkening around the ears and face mask, but there should be no other shading or marking. The Brown Burmese kitten is a pale chocolate or coffee color when born, but matures to its true color. The almost satin-like coat, short and close-lying, needs comparatively little grooming; just hard hand stroking, which they like, is sufficient to keep the coat shining.

The head should be wedge-shaped, rather than the shorter and blunter Siamese, with a distinct nose break. Viewed in profile the chin should show a strong lower jaw. The head should be slightly rounded, the roundness of head being more important in America. The ears should be spaced well apart, broad at the base and slightly rounded at the tip. Eyes should be a good, strong golden yellow, though they are often a greenish yellow shade.

The body should be long and slender, with legs slender in proportion to the body, the back ones a little longer than the front. The long tapering tail should not be too whip-like. The British cat should have small oval feet, but in America more rounded feet are demanded.

As with most breeds, breeding over time has resulted in further colors: these now include Chocolate (Champagne), Lilac (Platinum), Red, Tortoiseshell, Cream, Blue-Cream, Chocolate Tortie, and Lilac Tortie (Lilac-Cream).

Korat

This is another beautiful cat from Siam (Thailand). In this case we are now more certain of its origins. It has been known in Thailand for centuries, especially on the Korat plateau, but until recently it has been almost impossible for foreigners to

Above: the Blue Burmese appeared in a litter in Britain in 1955, and it was recognized as a breed in 1960. Sometimes the kittens have slight Tabby markings, but these disappear as the coat grows and becomes darker.

Left: the Red Burmese was developed by crossing Burmese with Red Tabbies and Red Point Siamese. Slight Tabby markings are often evident, but the coat should be light tangerine. The ears are a shade darker, while foot pads and nose leather are pink.

buy this much-prized and jealousy guarded animal. It was only in 1959 that the breed really became known outside Thailand when a pair was taken to America. They are now also recognized in Europe.

In its native country, where it is known as the Si-Sawat, the Korat has the reputation of bringing good luck to its owner. In fact its name means good fortune. Whether or not it brings you luck, it is certain to bring much pleasure, for the Korat makes a fine pet, being a good companion and often devoted to its owner. Although quiet and gentle in nature it is also playful and will easily learn such tricks as retrieving. A Korat will, however, demand much attention from its owner. Although the males make good parents and lead a domestic life of harmony with their own queen and kittens, they are sometimes less tolerant of other cats, and have a reputation for fighting.

Too much hustle and bustle seems to unnerve them: unless they have been accustomed to noise and activity as a kitten they could be too nervous to exhibit satisfactorily.

The breed is 'foreign' in type, medium build but muscular, with heart-shaped faces and large ears. The expressive eyes are blue in the kitten, but soon change through amber to a bright greenish gold.

It is, however, the coat which is most unusual and distinctive. It's glossy, with a unique coloring which looks silver-blue or slate-gray tipped with silver, depending on the angle from which it is admired. Hard hand stroking makes it shine even more.

Right: the Brown Burmese has the same foreign appearance as the Siamese, but the wedge-shaped head is not as long, and the ears are smaller. Body color is a dark seal-brown with ears and face mask slightly darker.

Below: Tortoiseshell Burmese are cats of unusual appearance, the coat being a mixture of red, brown and cream shades. Sometimes the legs or tail are a solid colour. Nose leather and foot pads may be plain or blotched. As with ordinary Tortoiseshell, this is an all-female breed.

Chapter

4 Longhaired Cats

Longhaired cats have been admired for centuries. However it was probably not until the 16th century that they were known in Europe — a French naturalist has been credited with bringing an Angora back from Turkey. The coats of these early longhairs were almost certainly less luxurious than those of today, though they were silky.

For some years all longhaired cats were known as Angoras because the first longhairs were brought back from Angora (now Ankara) in Turkey. Although they appeared in many colors, white tended to be the most popular.

It was the arrival of a new kind of longhair from Persia that changed everything. These had smaller ears and broader heads, longer, less silky fur, and a pronounced ruff. Again there were various colors, but this time it was black that society seemed to deem most desirable.

It didn't take long for cat fanciers to cross the Angora and Persian types, to produce a new strain also known as Persian. Then the Angoras faded into obscurity and may have become extinct had it not been for action taken by Ankara Zoo in re-establishing the breed.

Cat lovers will no doubt continue to refer to longhaired cats as Persians for some time to come, but in Britain they are now officially known as Longhairs, and both names are commonly used. It is, however, important to remember that there are other quite distinct breeds that have nothing to do with Persians.

Left: these two bundles of fluff are typical of the charm all longhairs possess at this age. Although they thoroughly enjoy the companionship of other kittens at this stage, as they mature they become less in need of cat companionship than the Orientals.

Far left: it is kittens like this Blue Longhair that tempt so many people when they come to choose a breed. Sometimes Blue kittens have slight Tabby markings when they are born, but these soon disappear.

Left: Cameo Longhairs, which are becoming more popular, are attractive cats. The lightly tipped coat imparts a shaded effect to the mature cat.

Below: for many years the Black Longhairs were very popular. It is very difficult to achieve a good strong black, but a good specimen looks superb.

Longhaired cats are decorative creatures with much visual appeal. When the Angoras were introduced they were regarded rather as an addition to decor, and could be seen in elegant drawing rooms sleeping on silk cushions.

Certainly you can be sure that a well-groomed longhair will be admired wherever you take it. But they have to be groomed.

Scrupulously clean and tidy animals though cats are, they cannot cope with the long flowing hair of modern breeds without help. They can't easily extricate chewing gum, or unravel the plugs and tangles that inevitably result from long hair.

A tatty longhair looks pathetic, and sometimes the fur gets into such a state that the only answer is to cut out tangles.

So no matter how taken you may be with the attractive pictures of these beautiful creatures, unless you have the time to groom your pet at least once a day, twice if you can, then it would be best to keep a shorthaired breed.

Start the grooming while the cat is still young and he will enjoy the beauty treatment, actually looking forward to it each day.

If you think you might want to go in for showing, then until you have gained experience with longhairs, you may find it best to avoid black or white varieties, for both can be difficult to keep in good color.

Black longhairs really should be a strong jet black, yet the color unfortunately tends to fade or turn a slightly rust color as a result of bleaching in the sun and as any cat owner will know, keeping them out of the sun is no easy matter. To add to your problems, rain or dampness can also affect the quality of the coat.

White coats aren't much easier to keep in pristine conditions. Unless your pet is kept scrupulously clean the coat is likely to become stained yellow in parts.

Despite these warnings, you should not be deterred from keeping what can be a quite spectacular pet. And despite the

need to keep *some* types out of the hot sun and free of dampness, there is nothing delicate about these hardy cats, and they should present no additional health problems apart from possible fur balls (see page 33). However, these are usually a result of neglected grooming.

Persian cats

There are many color forms, either selfs (that is all one color) or multicolored, but they all have long silky flowing coats and a ruff or frill round the neck, which, when brushed up, frames the head most attractively.

All cats in the Persian group should have a round, broad head with full cheeks and a broad muzzle, and a short, almost stubby nose, showing a distinct break between nose and skull. Small, well-shaped tufted ears and large bright eyes are desirable in all the various color forms.

The body on an ideal Persian should be long and low, with a deep chest and short, sturdy well-muscled legs. The tail should be short but thick with a tuft of long hair at the tip. There should also be hair tufts on the ears.

Black Longhair (Black Persian): This is one of the oldest pedigree Persian breeds. In 1871 it was described by the organizer of the first British Cat Show as 'the most sought-after and the most difficult to obtain'. It still isn't easy to buy a really good black, and it's amazing how even a single white hair shows up. Almost imperceptible stripes or bars can be detected in certain lights with some cats, and although these problems in no way spoil the animal as a pet, they are faults on the show bench.

Choosing a kitten can be a gamble too, for the coat often doesn't reveal its true potential until the cat is a year old, and sometimes a kitten with a rusty color turns out to have a superb jet black coat when it has matured.

White Longhair (White Persian): White Persians come in three types of eye coloring — blue-eyed, orange-eyed, and odd-eyed. The eye colour is particulary important with white cats, as it is genetically linked to certain defects, especially deafness.

Blue-eyed white longhaired cats are almost always deaf. This does not mean they will not make good pets, but it is important to be aware of the problem, for allowances will have to be made.

Odd-eyed cats have one blue and one orange, and deafness is not a problem.

Orange-eyed white longhairs used to be shown in the same class as the blue-eyed years ago, but it became clear that they were generally better specimens than the blue-eyed, and were recognized as a separate breed.

Blue Longhair (Blue Persian): The Blue Persian is a delightful cat and is justifiably one of the most popular longhairs. A wide variation is allowed in showing, and

Above: the Smoke Longhair, another distinctive breed is one of the progenitors of the Blue Smoke pictured on the opposite page. They are similar in all respects apart from color.

Above left: looking almost like a Chinese dragon, this Blue Smoke looks the aristocrat he is. This breed is the result of Smoke and Blue matings, and differs from the Smoke only in the tips of the hairs being blue instead of black.

Right: another delightful longhaired kitten — this one is a Cream. The light cream coloration tends to darken as a moult approaches; regular grooming should help to remove the old fur and maintain a good color.

Right: the Red Tabby Longhair can be a very striking cat, a good specimen having quite a strong red coloration rather than the orange of previous generations. In a good adult specimen the eyes are a deep copper.

Far right: this rather smug-looking cat is a Silver Tabby Longhair, an extremely beautiful cat. Good markings and color are not easy to produce, but the ground color should be silver with solid black Tabby markings.

tastes vary from country to country. The important criterion on the showbench is *evenness* of color, which may be anything from a delicate grayish-lavender to deep saphire, although grayish-blue is the most common.

This is another breed where color is uncertain in the kitten for many which show slight Tabby markings, especially on the head and legs, grow into superb cats of good color; equally some kittens which appear to have good color disappoint when they mature. Even buying an adult cat can be deceiving, for the coat sometimes darkens before being shed, and too much exposure to bright sunlight can give it a brownish hue.

Red Self Longhair (Solid Red Pesian): This uncommon breed is more of an orange than red, and it used to be known as the Orange Persian. The difficulty lies in achieving a solid color without the Tabby markings, especially on the face and tail. The ideal coat is an even rich orange-red without other markings; the eyes should be a deep copper color.

Cream Longhair (Cream Pesian): This should be a pale to medium clear cream without shading. Avoid any that tend to be too reddish. Their eyes should be a deep copper color.

You may find the color tends to darken a little before moulting but regular brushing and combing should help maintain an even clear color.

For genetic reasons there tend to be more male Creams than female.

Smoke Longhair (Black Smoke Persian): Smoke Persians are impressive creatures, with an appearance of almost aloof arrogance. It is a cat of contrasts, with the white coat tipped black. The feet should appear all black while the very long ruff and ear tufts should be silvery-white.

The effect of movement can be quite striking, as the white undercoat is revealed amid a flowing sea of fur. Regular daily grooming will help to prevent any old hair masking the shading.

This is another breed where the coloring is not obvious in very young kittens, which are usually born blue or black, with the undercoat only showing from about three weeks onwards. Even the young adult may not have a mature coat. Often it is not until the second adult coat that the clear silver ruff and ear tufts, and nice white chest and undercoat appears.

The Black Smoke has been known for more than a hundred years, and there is also a Blue Smoke. The only difference between the two is that instead of having black tips to the hairs they are blue. Although these are old breeds they are not common.

Siver Tabby Longhair (Silver Tabby Persian): This is an extremely distinctive and beautiful cat, showing clearly defined, dense black Tabby markings over a ground color of pale silver.

Again one must be careful not to be deceived when viewing kittens. Those which are nearly black at birth with markings only on the legs and sides often have really good markings by the time they are six months old. Equally, those born with distinct Tabby markings often fail to mature to perfect colors.

Brown Tabby Longhair (Brown Tabby Persian): The Brown Tabby Longhair is not as common as you might expect, mainly because there are not a great many breeders specializing in this cat, and breeding an animal with a good rich tawny sable background and nice dense black clearly-defined markings is not easy. The long flowing coat should be clearly marked on both body and tail. The British show bench also requires the facial markings to include delicate black pencilling with several swirls crossing the cheeks, narrow unbroken lines across the chest, and butterfly markings on the shoulders.

Red Tabby Longhair (Red Tabby Persian): The Red Tabby Persian is a striking cat, rich deep red in color. In the earlier days of the breed it was probably more orange. The Tabby markings may be either marbled or mackerel. The eyes are a deep copper color.

Chinchilla (Silver Persian): The Chinchilla is a striking white cat of exquisite beauty which has an endearing temperament and a confident personality. At first sight they appear to be self-colored cats, but close inspection shows that the tip of each hair on the head, back, flanks, ears and tail are tipped black. This gives the cat a shimmering appearance. Although the legs may be lightly shaded with a little tipping, the chin, ear tufts, chest and stomach must be pure white.

The expressive eyes are a distinctive

Previous page: the Shaded Cameo Longhair is a darker version of the Shell Cameo.

Right: this Blue White Longhair is rather rabbit-like in its markings, and, as with most longhairs, has an air of distinction.

Far right: the Chinchilla — surely one of our most magnificent cats. The dark outline to the eyes look as though eye-liner has been used.

Below right: this beautiful Odd-eyed White Longhair shows clearly the unusual effect of odd eyes. Blue-eyed white cats are quite often deaf, but if they have one orange eye the hearing is not affected. This makes the odd-eyed variety especially useful.

characteristic, colored emerald or blue-green, with the visible skin surrounding in dark brown. The contrast with the white makes it look as though an eye-liner has been used.

The Chinchilla tends to be smaller than other Persian types, and a fine-boned dainty appearance is encouraged in Britain, though in America a build rather like that of other Persians is preferred.

In North America and Australia the Shaded Silver Persian is recognized, and is another attractive cat very similar to the Chinchilla. The undercoat is a pale silver and the shading darker.

Tortoiseshell Longhair (Tortoisheshell Persian): This is an unusual cat. As its name implies it has Tortie markings, with patches of red, black and cream, but the fur is long. It is very difficult to breed this cat to order and nearly all are female, the occasional male almost invariably being sterile.

Many of the Tortoiseshell Longhairs produced have tabby marking or other faults which make them unsuitable for the show bench.

The long flowing coat should be well broken into rich patches of the three component colors, with no white hairs. Black should not be the predominant color. It is especially desirable that the colors are well broken on the face, and it is good to have a red or cream blaze running from nose to forehead. Eyes should be deep orange or copper.

Tortoiseshell and White Longhair (Calico Persian): This is a more striking cat than the ordinary Tortoiseshell Longhair, as it has white in addition to black, cream and red. The white is usually confined to the lower half of the cat. In North America it is known as the Calico Persian. Fertile males have been reported, but for practical purposes it should be regarded as an all-female breed. The markings required for showing vary slightly from country to country.

Blue Cream Longhair (Blue Cream Persian) This beautiful breed is the result of original crossings between blue and cream Persians, both of which have con-

tributed to a finely proportioned and marked cat. Over the years, however, ideals have diverged on opposite sides of the Atlantic, and in Britain the requirement is for a soft, dense and silky coat of blue and cream intermingled to give a whispy, smoky effect rather like shot silk. In North America, however, this is a fault, and distinct and separate patches of color are preferred. On both sides of the Atlantic the color of the large, round eyes should be a deep copper or dark orange.

These cats are almost invariably female. Males are sterile.

Bi-colored Longhair (Parti-colored Persian): This is another cat for which standards vary between countries. The long flowing silky coat may be any solid color and white — in Britain the white should not cover more than half the coat and the color not more than two-thirds.

Other Longhairs: Among the other Persian type that you may encounter are Blue Tabby, Cream Tabby, Peke-faced, Shell Cameo, Tortoiseshell Cameo, and Smoke Cameo (Red Smoke).

Persians with a Siamese influence

Seal Colorpoint (Seal Himalayan): Any cat with the form, structure and fur of the Persian with the markings and blue eyes of a Siamese is bound to be a striking cat. It sounds an improbable combination, but years of careful breeding have produced cats that incorporate some of the best features of both these impressive breeds.

Like many developments from established breeds, there was opposition from the purists at the beginning. There had been several attempts to cross Persians and Siamese with a view to producing a new hybrid breed, but most attempts succeeded only in raising a long-haired Siamese. Eventually such cats were recognized, though with the compromise that they were given a different name — Balinese (see page 92).

An American breeder trying to develop the Persian-Siamese cross met with such opposition from the Siamese lobby, who felt that it was unforgivable to obscure the smooth elegant lines of the Siamese with long fur, that she gave up her attempt.

However, an English breeder took up the challenge and attempted the cross. Then, unexpectedly, he was told of a stray 'long-haired Siamese'. It turned out to be more than that, for after several years of breeding he had succeeded in fixing a cat with all the proportions and coat of the Persian but with the distinctive markings of the Siamese.

Left: Bi-colored Longhairs (Parti-colored Persians) can be quite striking. The color can be any solid and white, with the markings extending on to the face, as this picture clearly shows. The black and white Bi-colors used to be known as Magpies.

Above: the Blue Cream Longhair is a handsome cat by any standard, although ideals vary on either side of the Atlantic. In Britain the color should be intermingled, but in North Americ more distinct patches are preferred.

Above: a Longhair with Siamese markings is bound to create attention. In the case of the Tortie Colorpoint (or Tortie Point Himalayan as it is also known) the effect is particularly unusual.

Right: the Maine Coon is an American breed originating in the Maine area of New England about the middle of the last century, and were thought by the local people to be the result of a cross between a cat and a raccoon. These cats make good, affectionate pets, and come in a range of colors.

In America the equivalent cats are known as Himalayans, but the basic requirements are broadly the same. The body should be of Persian type, with a short face and nose, and a definite 'break' or stop; cheeks should be full and the small tufted ears widely spaced. The long fur should be thick and soft, and the frill full. The large brilliant blue eyes should be round, but Oriental in shape like the Siamese.

The 'points' — face mask, ears, tail, legs and feet — are seal-brown in the basic type. But as one would expect, it was only a matter of time before other colors were established and recognized. These include Blue, Chocolate, Lilac, Red and Tortie.

Other longhaired cats

Maine Coon: About the middle of the last century, cats with long fur became established in Maine, New England. They had been brought back from Turkey by clipper and they were probably Angoras or a similar breed.

It was inevitable that these imported cats should breed with the local shorthaired cats, and it wasn't long before a new type of cat developed. It was called the Maine Coon, and before the days when we knew that crosses between such species were biologically impossible, many locals thought that these strong sturdy cats of the Angora type with thick coats, usually with Tabby markings, were cats crossed with raccoons.

The Maine Coon is a large, heavy cat, muscular and sturdy, but with the smallish tapering head and long-legged look of the Angora. The ears are large and the eyes, which may be green or some other color appropriate to the coat, are slightly slanting. The heavy shaggy coat, which is commonly Tabby in marking but may be any other color, is shorter than that of the Persians. It does not have the full ruff of the Persian. Their shorter coat is generally easier to maintain than the Persian's.

For many generations the Maine Coon, which is primarily a North American breed even today, has been sought after because of its affectionate nature. It has a reputation for shyness and is regarded as a good mouser.

Somali: The Somali is a longhaired version of the Abyssinian, and the type has been found for some years among normal litters in North America. But for a long time breeders did not own up to having longhairs among their kittens; it was thought that an abnormal length of hair among their stock would not benefit their reputations.

Eventually they were recognized as attractive cats in their own right, and in some North American shows they have their own classes.

The appearance of these cats is a little fox-like. They are generally larger than the normal Abyssinian, with a dense fine-textured silky coat which requires much less grooming than most longhairs. An occasional comb is generally sufficient to keep it in condition. Although the coat is sometimes thinner on the shoulders, a full ruff and good ear tufts are desirable. They make affectionate and lively pets.

Chapter

5 Shorthaired Cats

Many people regard most of our shorthaired cats as ordinary, without any real breeding or ancestry. Nothing could be further from the truth, for shorthairs are noble breeds which have their own unique histories, their own individual characteristics and qualities, and many undoubted merits.

Even the brown Tabby found in so many homes as the family pet, or in offices and factories as the resident 'mouser', has as much history as any other breed. Of course most of the Tabbies we see do not come of pedigree stock, but remember that many natural breeds, Siamese or Birmans for instance, were only pedigree once they were bred and recorded in a controlled manner. So it is with many other of our domestic cats; there are the natural uncontrolled Tabbies, black cats and Tortoiseshells, and there are those which have had their mates chosen for them and become pedigrees.

Shorthaired cats have the merit of requiring less attention with regard to grooming; a brush and comb once a week will keep that bloom on their coat.

British Shorthairs are usually less mischievous than the Oriental breeds, but they are active cats that need a lot of outdoor exercise. They really need a garden and are seldom happy if they have to lead an indoor existence.

Shorthairs are usually divided into two broad groups — British Shorthairs and Foreign Shorthairs. The terms say nothing of the origins of these cats — they are used only to describe the shape and build.

Left: the Tabby is one of our oldest shorthair breeds, and these cats are widespread. The most common form is the Brown Tabby, but there are other less frequently seen colors, such as this Red Tabby seen here enjoying the freedom they like so much.

Above: black cats have always created feelings of love or fear, and have been the subject of many superstitions. In fact they are lovely creatures, full of dignity. A good specimen looks really impressive, although it is not easy to achieve a jet black coat.

Left: although odd-eyed white cats look very strange, they have the merit of not carrying the deafness factor which is often present in white cats with two blue eyes. Although deaf cats can make affectionate pets, they do need special attention.

British shorthairs

The British Shorthair has a powerful well-muscled body of medium length, with a broad deep chest, and large round head set on a short thick neck. The cheeks are full and well developed, and their small neat ears are spaced well apart, slightly rounded at the tips. Short but sturdy legs should be well boned with small oval feet. The shortish tail, carried almost level with the back, should be thick at the base, tapering to a point at the tip.

The original stock taken to North America by early settlers was the same as the British cat. Over the years there have been slight changes which have become fixed and recognized. The American Shorthair (or Domestic Shorthair as it is also known) is a sturdy cat with firmly boned legs and a tail which is thick at the base. The large full-cheeked head has more of an oblong appearance than the British cat, and the muzzle is squarer, the chin well developed. The nose is slightly longer than the British version, and the short thick coat is somewhat less luxurious.

White Shorthair: White cats in various countries have been regarded as bringing either bad luck or good fortune, depending on the fashion of the time. But for many people white cats are beautiful creatures, and they are not as difficult to keep clean as one might expect. Apart from a little attention to the tail end to prevent any yellow staining becoming too ingrained, you will find the fastidiousness of the cat will maintain a very presentable coat for the world to admire.

A good White Shorthair should have a pure white coat, with no yellowing or creaminess. But don't be deterred by a tiny smudge of dark hair on the head of a kitten, for this can be a reassuring sign in a blue-eyed kitten. They all have blue eyes to start with, though probably the deeper the color the more likely they are to stay blue. The question of eye color assumes considerably more sig-

Below: the Silver Tabby is one of the most handsome shorthairs. The background color should be a clear silver, with no sign of white, and the markings should be dense black. Any brown markings, or white on the chin, are considered bad faults on the show bench.

Right: the British Blue is a cuddly-looking cat, with a nice chubby body and almost plush-like bluish-gray coat. It also has a very good nature, being placid, gentle and affectionate. The equivalent cat in North America is known as the Blue Exotic Shorthair.

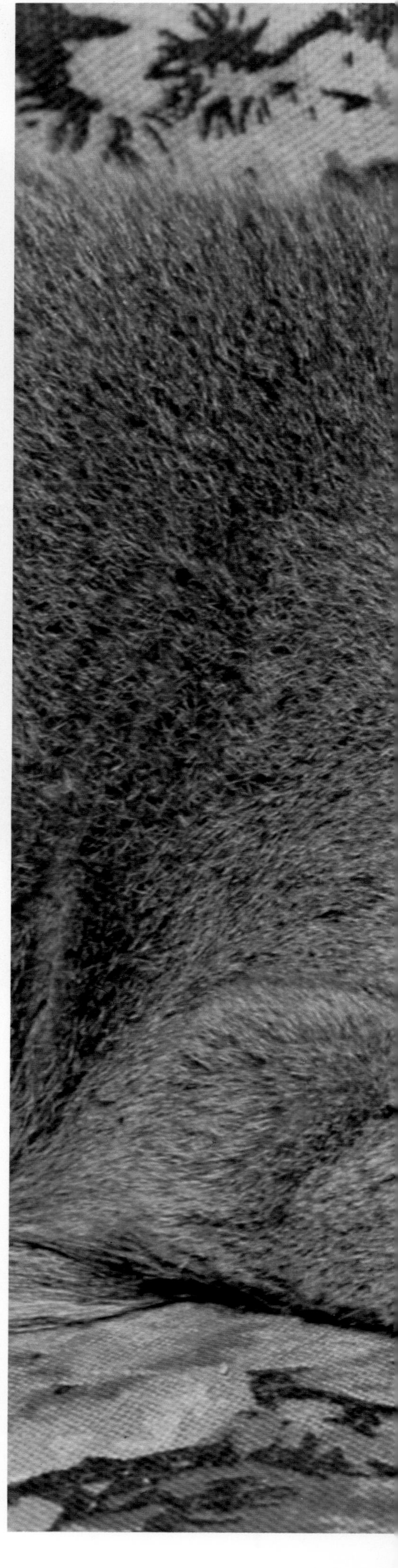

nificance in white cats than other colors, because there is a genetic connection between blue-eyed cats and deafness. Such cats live quite happy lives, but they are disadvantaged, and you will need to make many more adjustments and allowances for such a pet.

Not all white cats have blue eyes — some have orange, others even have odd eyes (one blue, one orange). Provided just one eye is orange hearing should be satisfactory, and of course if both are orange you need have no worries about deafness.

Amazingly, if a blue-eyed white cat has just a couple of colored hairs, such as those already mentioned hearing should be normal. And as these few dark hairs usually disappear in the adult cat, you can be fairly confident of a blue-eyed white cat with good hearing.

Deaf cats can be particularly affectionate, being most appreciative of human company, and they really enjoy physical contact through stroking. You will also be able to train him to understand simple commands by signs such as pointing, and by vibrations such as tapping. The main worry with such cats is their total oblivion to traffic dangers, and you should really be prepared to keep them within the home and garden. The garden should be adequately fenced — but it's not easy to do this.

Black Shorthair: Like white cats, black cats generate strong feelings of love or hate. Some people think of them as lucky and others as unlucky and evil-looking.

Good black cats are not as easy to come by as one might expect, for it is no easy matter to achieve a jet black coat. Even if bred pure black it can be discolored by too much sun. Faint tabby markings or a brownish discoloration on kittens, however, may well grow out.

The other major problem if you set your mind on the show bench is the eyes, which are expected to be orange or deep copper. This is asking a lot when you consider that the natural color is green, which will always predominate.

You will find the coat will shine nicely if you give it a good polish with a chamois leather, but of course it won't do anything to mask bad coloring.

British Blue: In America, what is probably the same cat is known as the Blue Exotic Shorthair. It is a magnificent cat: strongly built and really sturdy, with a fine short, almost plush-like coat of an even bluish-gray, and with large copper, orange or yellow eyes.

A characteristic of a good specimen is a nice even coloration, without any shad-

ing towards the roots. In the past a darker slate color was probably preferred, but today's cats are paler.

The British Blue is placid and gentle as well as affectionate and intelligent.

Cream Shorthair: Cream Shorthairs are very attractive cats, but not common because it is difficult to achieve good color without traces of white or barring showing through. Barred kittens may lose the marking as they age, but there is a risk of it reappearing during extremes of temperature.

Brown Tabby: Perhaps the best known of all cats is the Tabby, and it plays a significant part in the ancestry of many other breeds. This is obvious in the kittens of many other breeds, where the tabby markings show through until they disappear with age. They also have a knack of coming through as a fault in mature cats of other breeds. Indeed it is the preoccupation of many breeders to eliminate any traces of Tabby markings from their particular breed.

The origins of the tabby have been lost in history, but it is likely that it was introduced into Britain by the Romans, and then it was only a matter of time before it made its way from there to America and Australia. It is thought that the word Tabby comes from an Arabic word *attabi*, which was the word used to describe a wavy-lined silk or taffeta.

The Tabby pattern has many variations, however, and apart from good and bad specimens of the normal blotched or marbled Tabby, there are two other most attractive patterns — the lovely mackerel pattern and an attractive spotted kind, though the latter is now generally regarded as a separate breed. The mackerel markings are, as the name suggests, reminiscent of a mackerel, with dark bands or stripes down the sides and a central stripe running along the backbone. These should be definite stripes and not break up into dots. The pattern is sometimes known as the tiger pattern.

The Brown Tabby should have a ground color of rich sable or brown, with dense black markings which show no sign of mingling with the background.

As with other Tabbies, the markings are clear at birth.

The most widely seen marking is of course the standard marbled version which has three solid stripes down the spine, a butterfly pattern on the shoulders and a dark M-shaped mark on the head, with dark whorles on the flanks. A pair of unbroken narrow lines down the chest are popularly known as mayoral chains. A well-marked specimen also has clear pencil markings on the face and clearly defined rings round the eyes.

Silver Tabby: The Silver Tabby is considered by some to be a more beautiful cat

Above: Red Tabbies are attractive cats, but it is difficult to achieve a strong color. More male than female kittens are born, although females are not uncommon.

Right: one of our most common cats is the Brown Tabby, yet good pedigree specimens are uncommon. It is not an easy cat to breed true to type with a perfectly patterned coat, and very skilful breeding is required. Mackerel pattern Tabbies are also very attractive.

than the Brown — certainly its clear silver ground color and dense black markings make it a lovely looking cat.

Do not worry if kittens that were clearly marked at birth look rather grayish as the fur grows: the color should be established by the time they are about three months old.

Red Tabby: This is less common than the other tabbies, mainly because it is difficult to breed a good color. Ideally the background color should be a deep orange-red, not sandy or ginger, with darker red markings, matched with deep orange eyes, though they may also be hazel.

Tortoiseshell Shorthair: Most people know the Tortoiseshell, a spectacular and much loved cat, with its blotches of black, red and cream. These cats are sometimes known in North America by the rather charming name of Clouded Tigers.

Tortoiseshells are unpredictable cats to breed, for they are usually females, any males are almost invariably sterile.

The Tortie is a good example of how loosely the term 'breed' is used, for like several other 'breeds' it is more technically a cross-bred, as it is not possible to mate two of a like kind to procreate more of the same kind. However, common usage is what counts, and it is convenient to think of such animals as true breeds.

One of the reasons this old breed has always been popular is its usually pleasant disposition, and Tortoiseshells tend to make ideal pets.

Tortoiseshell and White (Calico) Shorthair: The Tortoiseshell and White Shorthair is known as the Calico cat in America, and being an old breed it has acquired other names over the years, including Spanish Cat. They are not in fact a purely Spanish phenomenon, and are known in various parts of the world. Japanese sailors used to take them to sea because they thought they would ward off storms and evil spirits.

In appearance they are like the Tortoiseshell, but the lower half is splashed with white.

This is a female-only breed.

Blue Cream Shorthair: This is another female breed, the coloring being sex linked in a similar way to the Tortoiseshell. It is an uncommon but very handsome cat of much charm.

The short fine coat is a mixture of gray-blue and cream, but how they are mixed depends on which side of the Atlantic you live. In North America, clearly defined patches are necessary while in Britain a mingled coat is favored, the two colors attractively intermingled without any distinct patches.

Spotted Shorthair: This is really a modified form of tabby marking, and in the very early cat shows were exhibited as such. Now they are treated as a distinct breed. There are of course spotted cats in various parts of the world, and the British Spotted Shorthair is surprisingly uncommon considering so many of the domestic cat's wild relatives have spotted coats. The spots need not be round, but they must be clearly defined and not form

Above: the Silver Spotted Shorthair is still quite unusual, even though they were exhibited in the very early cat shows. They used to be shown as a variety of Tabby, but are now treated as a distinct variety and have their own standard. The spots or blotches should be distinct and not merge into each other.

Left: Tabby cats are agile, and delight in climbing trees, peering at passers-by in a searching manner.

stripes or bars, or appear as broken stripes. They can be any color.

Bi-color (Parti-colored) Shorthair: A well marked Bi-color can be a very impressive animal, with the bold contrast of color and white. The black and whites were once known affectionately as Magpies, and this was the main color combination. Now there are various other colors.

Up to two thirds of the coat should be colored. and not more than half white. The face should be patched, ideally with a white blaze down the centre.

Foreign Shorthairs

Foreign Shorthairs are not necessarily from far-off lands. The word is intended to describe a *type* of cat, which looks very different from the stocky British breeds. The foreign shape is much sleeker and more streamlined in appearance, with slimmer bodies, long tails and slender legs. The heads tend to be more wedge-shaped, broad at the top, narrowing to the muzzle. The ears are also rather large, pointed and pricked. Eyes are more oval-shaped and slanting than the round type of the British breeds.

Although individual breeds vary, as a group, they tend to need companionship more than other cats — whether human or animal.

Practically all of them are easy to groom, hand stroking and perhaps a rub with a chamois leather usually being sufficient to maintain an attractive sheen.

Abyssinian: There is no shortage of theories about the origins of the Abyssinian, the more romantic ones sadly lack-

ing in credibility. But even the more probable ones are fascinating.

A book published in 1874 claims that a Mrs. Barrett-Lennart brought a cat called Zula back from Abyssinia when a British Expedition returned. However a picture of Zula published six years later shows a cat that in no way can be said to resemble the animal we call an Abyssinian today.

Another theory makes the trip in reverse, describing how the first one in Britain happened to be taken to Abyssinia by an army officer's wife after the Italo-Abyssinian War.

Many owners like to think that the Abyssinian is descended from the ancient cats of Egypt, but this theory can be dismissed.

The truth is probably far more mundane. From time to time kittens are born with Abyssinian type coats to chance matings between ordinary Tabby cats. These have the special 'ticked' coat which makes the Abyssinian so distinctive, and by careful breeding the ticked coat can be established as a type. That's not the whole story of course, as the Abyssinian is foreign in type. Somewhere along the line there must have been crossings with cats of this build. Whether all this was by chance or design is difficult to say now, but the breed was first recognized and listed in 1882 and there is on record a photograph taken in 1903 which shows the cat as we know it today. But more importantly, the only entries in the National Cat Society's stud books at the turn of the century were listed as 'pedigree unknown'.

The ticked coat may of course be a throwback to early and more primitive cats, but the development of the breed is almost certainly British. How it then got the name Abyssinian is open to speculation.

Whatever the origins of the Abyssinian, it is a highly desirable and distinctive

Left: although only a few cats like to swim, water holds a fascination for them and they will sometimes fish with their paws. Garden pools are usually the target, but this Red Tabby is investigating the local stream.

breed. The original color was a ruddy-brown, but there are now a number of other colors, including red.

Young kittens may not show the distinctive ticking, which only becomes obvious at about two months.

The Abyssinian has a slightly wild look about it, yet this affectionate and intelligent cat can make a marvellous pet. It has the cute tendency to pick things up with its paws, and is the sort of cat which puts a paw round its owner's neck in affection. In return they like lots of attention coupled with freedom — they seem unhappy if too confined.

Besides the standard or Ruddy Abyssinian, there are red, blue, cream, chocolate and lilac versions.

Russian Blue: Even if we have our doubts about the so-called Russian link, it is sometimes pleasant to speculate on the origin of the breed. The Russian Blue is one of those cats with several theories attached to its name. The idea that they were a gift from a Russian Czar can be discounted fairly easily; although gray blue cats probably did occur in Russia, it's also fairly certain they occurred as mutations in several parts of the world.

These occasional mutations would not of course necessarily result in established breeds and the Russian Blue we know today is almost certanly due to the intervention of man. In fact at one stage British and Scandinavian breeders were introducing Siamese mates, although the Siamese influence is now out of favour and the emphasis is on a cat that is perhaps more British in outline.

Today's cat is graceful, with a long body, slender legs, and dainty oval feet. The gray-blue coat has a silvery sheen. The short, thick, and very fine fur is almost plush-like. The short, wedge-shaped head is made especially attractive with vivid green slanting eyes, and long large, wide-based ears that are so thin they are nearly transparent.

The Russian Blue is a quiet cat, sometimes thought of as a little shy, but it is gentle and can become very attached to its owner as a loyal and friendly pet.

Above: the Russian Blue can become very attached to its owner, and is well suited to life in a flat, having a quiet nature. The ears are an unusual feature with comparatively little fur covering and are so thin that they are almost transparent.

Right: how the Abyssinian received its name is open to speculation, but the breed may well be a throwback to more primitive cats. Whatever the genetic background, the breed was developed in Britain. Abyssinians make marvellous pets, being affectionate and intelligent, but they also appreciate a good degree of freedom.

Chapter

6 Some Unusual Breed

The cats in this chapter are unusual in different ways. Some, such as the Japanese Bobtail, are both unusual and rare; others like the Rex cats are more common but still strange creatures by any standards. Yet others, such as the Birman, more romantically known as the Sacred Cat of Burma, have an interesting and fascinating history.

Several of the breeds included are mutations that in nature would have been fatal — cats without adequate fur would not last long without protection, for instance, and Ragdolls lack the fear instinct and drive that would be essential for survival in the wild. This invariably leads to debate among cat lovers about the desirability of perpetuating what are in effect abnormalities. On the other hand, most of our pets are not kept in a natural environment and do not have to fend for themselves, and they can lead happy lives whilst giving great pleasure to their owners.

The Manx is one example where the mutation is clearly a serious genetic defect, yet the breed was strong enough to survive over a long period without special protection. Those that live make charming pets, but there is a high mortality rate among new-born kittens.

Although the cats in this chapter are sure to create attention, they should never be bought just for novelty — only if their own qualities fulfil your ideals in a pet.

Left: the Birman, also known as the Sacred Cat of Burma, should not be confused with the Burmese, which is a shorthaired cat. A distinctive feature of the Birman is the white paws. The two cats pictured here are a Blue Point and a Seal Point.

Above: the Devon Rex was at first thought to be genetically similar to the Cornish Rex (opposite), but proved not be so. The short, fine wavy coat is harsher than that of the Cornish Rex. It makes an excellent pet, and is very suitable for flat dwellers.

Left: the Cornish Rex is an intriguing cat, with a curly coat that lacks guard hairs. This short and distinctive coat should be thick, plushy and wavy, especially on the back. The parents of the first Rex kitten were ordinary short-coated cats from Cornwall in England.

Rex cats

Rex cats are quite a recent development: consequently we know a lot about their evolution, unlike many other breeds whose ancestral derivation are now lost in history.

The type you are most likely to encounter are the Devon and Cornish Rex Cats. The story begins at the end of the Second World War, when a German Rex seems to have occurred as a chance mutation in Berlin. The descendants of this cat were used to establish the Rex strain in America, and it may in fact be the same genetically as the Cornish Rex. The Cornish Rex was a mutation which occurred on a farm in Cornwall, England, in 1950. We don't know who the father was, but the mother was a Tortoiseshell and White Shorthair. Unlike the rest of the litter which had straight coats, this mutation had a curly coat and whiskers. The offspring of this cat produced either curly-coated or plain kittens.

Two Cornish Rex were sent to America at the end of the 1950s, about the same time as a mutation appeared in Oregon, United States of America, with similar characteristics.

Back in England in 1960, another mutation occurred with a Rex coat, this time in the neighboring county of Devon. It seemed natural to assume they were the same genetically, but this proved not to be the case: they were developed in Britain as two distinct breeds.

Both Cornish and Devon Rex cats have a distinctive appearance quite unlike any other breed. Both have a silky, curly fur, although that of the Devon Rex is slightly harsher. As always, different color forms followed, and there are now many different kinds, including a Siamese type known as the Si-Rex.

Rex cats are among the easiest to groom, they don't shed hairs, and they make ideal pets. They are affectionate animals, having bright and outgoing personalities.

The Cornish Rex has a medium wedge-shaped head, with a flat skull and straight nose. The Devon Rex has fuller cheeks and a pronounced break or stop to the nose, and a short muzzle.

Manx

Most people know what the distinctive Manx looks like. Their main characteristic is, of course, their tail — or rather the lack of one. In a good specimen it is entirely absent, and the cat is known as a 'rumpy': but there are also 'stumpies', which have a short stump or a tail. It has given rise to a number of legends over the years, but it should not be regarded merely as a curiosity, as it has a very desirable temperament which makes it a good pet. Manx are playful cats, willing to retrieve small balls, and they have an affectionate nature. They are also easily trained, and it is not difficult to get them to come when you call their name or to walk them on a lead. They are adaptable cats, and show little sign of nervousness.

Another feature is their soft voice, which is sometimes more like a squeak.

In a 'rumpy' you should be able to feel an actual depression where the tail should be, but sometimes there is a small tuft of fur, although it should not contain any cartilage or bone. The rump should be nicely rounded.

It is not only the lack of tail which is unusual — the double coat is also quite

Right: it was only a matter of time before breeders extended the color range of Rex cats, and now many types are available. Even though the cat in the picture looks very different from our popular Tabby, the markings are nevertheless there in this Tabby Rex.

Below: this Si-Rex looks almost like a small lamb with its pale curly coat. As the name implies, it is a Rex with Siamese markings — complete with blue eyes. It demonstrates clearly what can be achieved once a new type has been established.

distinctive, being soft and open and feeling rather like a rabbit's fur. It also walks with a rabbity gait, due to its high hindquarter with a deep flank, and the comparatively short back.

Manx are not easy to breed, and it should not be attempted without careful thought and research. The difficulty lies in the fact that the same genetic defect responsible for the absent tail can also affect other parts of the spinal column, and there is a significant risk of deformed kittens, many of which soon die. This is only a problem if Manx is mated with Manx. The offspring of two Manx may also be sterile. 'Stumpies' do not have the same problems.

A Manx mated with a tailed cat that has Manx in its genetic make-up may produce 'rumpies'.

We know today that the Manx is just a genetic mutation.

There are two variations of the story telling how the Manx lost its tail back in the days of Noah. One version has it that the cat left it almost too late to get on the ark and Noah, anxious to leave, slammed the door shut on his tail. Another version has it that the cat was so eager to the leave the ark when the waters subsided that he tried to jump out of a window, but a dog snapped at her and bit off her tail.

There are other stories equally far-fetched. One tells of a female who bit off the tails of her kittens in order that they would not be killed for their tails which were used as plumes in the helmets of Manx warriors.

In fact tail-less cats were not confined to the Isle of Man, for Charles Darwin reported seeing them in Malaya, Burma, China and Japan. It is not known whether the Manx was imported to the Isle of Man or arose there independently, but it is likely that the small size of the island resulted in close inbreeding which helped to establish the breed.

Manx come in most of the usual colors and markings.

Hairless cats

Hairless cats often generate heated discussion about the merits of fixing such traits. Some cat lovers feel it is wrong to breed from what would be fatal mutations in nature. Hairless cats are not normally recognized by cat authorities, though in some countries the Sphynx is acknowledged.

There have been several instances of hairless breeds, including a hairless form of Siamese, and the Mexican Hairless

Cat, which is presumed extinct.

The Sphynx, which is sometimes known as the Canadian Hairless, orginated in Ontario in 1966. A black and white house cat gave birth to a male hairless kitten and the resulting cat was not dissimilar to the Mexican Hairless. Although the kittens have fine short hair, most of this disappears by the time they are adult, apart from certain points such as the face, feet and tail. Males, however, have a fairly strong hair growth covering the testicles.

Egyptian Mau

The cat was for a long time a sacred animal in Egypt, and there can be little doubt that this was because of their usefulness in controlling vermin in the granaries and elsewhere.

The word they used for cat was Mu, and we know something of its features from various sculptures and paintings which have survived from ancient Egypt. Certain breeders in both America and Britain attempted to recreate the Egyptian Mau, and although the results for the two countries are slightly different, both versions are attractive cats. The American breed was established from cats which originally came from Cairo, while in Britain they were bred mainly from Tabbies of a foreign type, which were the result of trying to breed Tabby Point Siamese.

The Egyptian Mau now comes in several colour forms, but ideals are different on opposite sides of the Atlantic. Because of the Siamese influence in the British cat there is a more pronounced 'foreign' look, and Oriental eyes. The British version should have a mark like a scarab beetle between the ears.

Japanese Bobtail

The Japanese Bobtail is a very old breed. It appears in many Japanese paintings, and pictures of the Bobtail decorate an old temple in Tokyo. Yet surprisingly it is only comparatively recently that is has been bred outside Japan.

The Japanese Bobtail is a most distinctive cat which, although well-muscled and strongly built, is still quite slim. The head is almost triangular in shape with eyes that have definite Japanese characteristics.

The most distinctive feature is, of course, its tail. This is usually about 100mm (4in) long uncurled, although it appears to be only half this length.

Above: the Sphynx, being practically hairless, naturally attracts a lot of attention whenever it is seen. The breed is probably similar to the extinct Mexican Hairless cats, which were last recorded in the 1900s.

Left: Manx cats are recognized wherever they are seen. There are two types, known as 'rumpies' and 'stumpies'. The 'rumpy' has a depression or tuft of fur where the tail should be, while the stumpy (pictured here) has a short stumped tail.

Because the hair on it grows out in all directions the tail has a pom-pom effect.

The coloring may be self (all one shade), patched or tortoiseshell.

Scottish Fold

The Scottish Fold has lop ears, and falls into the same category as hairless cats, generating the same heated arguments about whether such mutations should be perpetuated and encouraged.

There are records from the 18th century of such cats being seen in China, but the mutation seems extremely rare. It is known that one was brought back from China during the 19th century, but it was not until 1938 that scientists found another example.

The Scottish Fold originated in Scotland in 1961. The ears fold forward and downwards. Similar mutations have occurred in Belgium and Germany.

Turkish Swimming Cat

Anyone who has tried to bath a cat will probably be very surprised to hear of one that actually likes water — and even goes swimming for the pleasure of it. When the Turkish Swimming Cats were introduced into Britain and America they generated much interest. It wasn't until the mid 1950s that they appeared in Europe.

They have long hair that is chalky white with auburn patches on the face and an auburn tail with light and dark rings. The ears should be white, matching a white blaze up the face. The inside of the ears, the paw pads and the nose tip should be pale pink.

Sacred Cat of Burma

The Sacred Cat of Burma, or Birman, is an impressive creature with its long pale-colored coat and contrasting face mask, ears, tail and legs, and most distinctive white paws that look like mittens. The white of the mittens is extended up the back of the hind legs.

The Birman looks very much like a Colorpoint apart from its white feet, but it is a distinct breed. It is also important not to confuse them with the Burmese, which are shorthaired cats.

The breed's romantic name arises from its alleged descent from the temple cats of Burma. It found its way to Britain and America by way of France. A pair were given to two soldiers as a token of thanks for their services during a rebellion. Although one died on the way back to

France, the other was pregnant and lived to establish the breed.

According to legend, cats of this type were kept for centuries in the temples of the East, and just like the Siamese they also have legends describing the origin of their distinctive features. As with most legends, slight variations have sprung up over the years.

The white feet and blue eyes are explained this way: hundreds of years ago there was an old Kittah priest who kept a white cat called Sinh, which he regarded as his oracle. They sat together in the temple before the statue of a blue-eyed golden goddess. The temple was under threat because their country had been invaded.

Depending on which version you care to believe, the priest either died or was killed by the invaders. Then at the moment when the old man's spirit left him, his faithful friend leapt up to the sacred throne, resting all four paws on the dead priest's silvery beard. Dramatically, the white fur on the cat's back turned into the golden color of the statue, and his eyes turned the same dazzling sapphire blue as those of the golden goddess. His ears, face, legs and tail all changed to the color of the fertile earth, and only where his feet remained in contact with the old man's beard did the fur remain white to signify his purity.

Witnessing such a miracle the monks were strengthened enough to defeat the enemy.

The story goes on to say that for another week Sinh sat by his master's throne, unwilling to eat or drink, and then he died. But that was not the end of the miracle, for from that time on all the cats in the temple also had the same unique coloring.

The base color is in fact not gold but a creamy-gold or beige with a slightly golden tinge. The principal type is the seal point, which has typical brown seal markings, but other kinds are available such as Chocolate, Lilac and Blue Point.

Balinese

Balinese are really longhaired Siamese, but because many purists thought it was wrong to give the name Siamese to a cat that lacked the true Oriental look of the shorthaired cat, the new breed was given a different name.

At first glance they look like the Colorpoints, which also have the same 'point' markings as the Siamese. The Balinese, however, lacks the ruff of the Colorpoints and is a sleeker cat, muscular yet elegant in build.

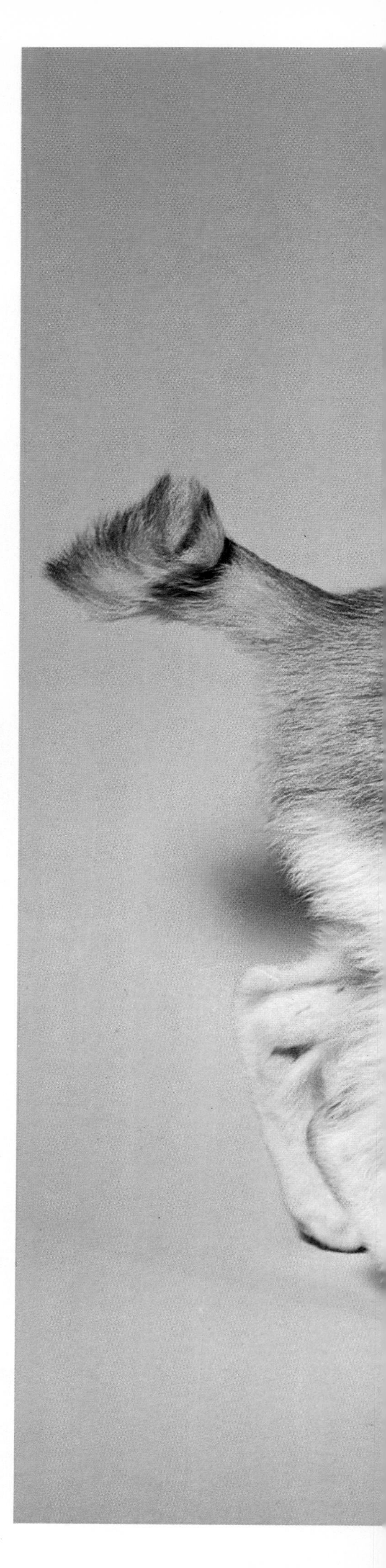

Above and right: the Japanese Bobtail has been known in Japan for centuries, but it is only in the last ten years that they have been bred outside that country. Although there are similarities with the 'Stumpy' Manx, they are not related in any way.

Above: the Sacred Cat of Burma, which is also known as the Birman, is a lovely cat with a dignified look. Legend has it that they are descended from the cats that guarded the temples of Burma, but whatever their origins they are distinctive and beautiful cats.

Right: as anyone who has tried to bath a cat will know, it is an unusual one that actually likes going for a dip, but the Turkish Swimming Cat really does seem to enjoy swimming. They used be called Van cats, because they originated from that part of Turkey.

The longish coat is fine and silky, with an even tone of ground color, which should contrast well with the darker points and mask. The main type is the Seal Point, with a body color of warm pale fawn to cream, and lighter shading on the underparts.

There are other colors, including the Blue Point, which has a cold bluish-white body, shading to white on the underparts, with blue points. The nose leather and paw pads are slate, unlike the rich seal-brown of the Seal Point.

The Chocolate Point has an ivory body color with no shading underneath, and points of a warm milk chocolate shade, the nose leather and pads being cinnamon-pink.

The Lilac or Frost Point Balinese should be glacial white without any shading, and have a pinkish-gray mask and points. Lavender-pink is the right color for paw pads and nose leather.

Don't be surprised if the coat tends to darken as the cat ages, but it should not affect the contrast bewtween body color and points. The eyes of all types should be a vivid blue.

Balinese make intelligent, attractive and amiable pets.

Ragdoll

This very unusual breed was developed in California about ten years ago, and its breeding has been carefully controlled. Although it is unlikely that many readers will come across this unique cat, it has to be mentioned because of its amazing disposition. It seems to know no fear, and is so placid and limp when picked up that it feels like a rag doll. In fact they lack most of the characteristics of the normal feline temperament, being dependent on their owner for protection.

The breed stems from a white Persian which was severly injured in a road accident. All her kittens seemed to show the same unique characteristics.

They look rather like a Birman, but with thicker fur and heavier body. The kittens, which are white when born, do not attain full color for about 18 months.

Index

Page numbers in italics refer to illustrations

Acknowledgements

The publishers would like to thank the following photographic agencies for their kind permission to reproduce photographs in this book:

Bruce Coleman Limited: Front and end papers, 2/3, 6/7, 8/9, 10 (top left and top right), 12, 13, 14 (top), 15, 16, 17, 18, 21, 22, 23 (top left and right), 25 (bottom right), 26/27, 30, 31, 32, 33, 34, 35, 36, 37, 38/39, 40, 42, 44/45, 45, 48/49, 49, 50, 51, 52, 53, 54/55, 56, 57, (top left), 58, 59 (top and bottom right), 60, 62/63, 64 (top right and bottom right), 66/67, 68, 69, 72, 73, 74, 74/75, 77, 80/81, 84/85, 86, 88, 90, 91, 92, 92/93, 94 and 95.

Zefa Picture Library (U.K.) Limited: 4/5, 11, 14, (bottom left), 19, 20, 24, 25, 27, 28/29, 41, 43, 46, 47, 57, 61, 65, 67 (bottom right), 70/71, 76, 78, 79, 82, 83, 87 and 89.

Front cover: Zefa Picture Library (U.K.) Limited

Back Cover: Bruce Coleman Limited